How to Be Your Own Boss

Your Road Map to Self-Employed Success

How to take your talents and skills into the marketplace as an entrepreneur and launch your own business.

Eric Deeter

Copyright Eric Deeter © 2014

All rights reserved. No part of this book may be reproduced or transmitted in any form or by any means without the written permission of the author, including reproductions for non-commercial use. This book makes reference to trademarks for editorial purposes only; the author makes no commercial claims on their use. Nothing contained herein is intended to express judgment on or affect the validity of the legal status of any term or word as a trademark, service mark or other proprietary mark.

DISCLAIMER:

This book intends to be a guide for entrepreneurs and those considering entrepreneurship. It is based on the author's 20 years of experience as a self-employed owner of a service business. It is not intended to give comprehensive instructions for setting up or running a business, nor a substitute for legal or other expert advice. While every effort has been made to ensure this book is accurate and up to date, mistakes or inaccuracies may well exist. The author accepts no liability or responsibility for any loss or damage caused, or thought to be caused, by following the advice in the book and recommends that you use it only in conjunction with other trusted sources of information.

All monetary references are in US dollars.

Original title: Stop Your Paycheck Addiction

First Printing June 2014

ISBN: **978-1986130219**DEDICATION

To Brenda

My partner in life and in business.

You make me a better man.

Without you this book would never

have been possible.

CONTENTS

	Introduction	i
1	The Start of Addiction	1
2	Think Like an Owner	12
3	Making Money	33
4	Take Your Skills to Market	57
5	Basic Marketing	76
6	Relationship Marketing	96
7	Guerrilla Marketing	114
8	Start Up Money	127
9	Manage Your Money	138
10	Contain and Control	156
11	The Powers That Be	177
12	Bring Your A-Game	190
13	Growing Pains	206
14	Your Main Asset	223

Introduction

Experience is an effective teacher. The lessons go deep when you learn from experience.

Take, for example, my first lesson on electricity. I was 18 months old. Naturally curious, I wondered: why do certain appliances work when attached to a wall outlet? And the bobby pin I found looked like a good discovery tool.

It's my earliest memory. I can still see the outlet. An end table and lamp are to my right, beside the sofa. My mom is on the sofa, holding a used-up light bulb in a sock, darning the toe. (Yes, Google explains *darning* if you're unfamiliar with the term.) I pull open the bobby pin. The lamp is plugged into the bottom outlet. So I push my improvised tool into the top outlet.

Sparks fly. The lamp flicks off. I jerk back and my head hits the table. I cry. Mom leaps from the couch and grabs me. And I live to tell about it.

My first electrical lesson was successful and effective. I learned bare metal and electricity are a bad combination. And that lesson went deep.

I'm sure you have your own stories of experiences survived and lessons learned. Your experiences and lessons are more complex and abstract as you get older. But the curriculum is similar. You get burned unexpectedly because you don't know any better. You probably know these lessons by their common name: The School of Hard Knocks.

The School of Hard Knocks exacts a steep price for its lessons. On one hand, I wouldn't trade some of those lessons for any amount of money. But on the other hand, I'd also spend any amount of money to never go through them again.

They say bad decisions make good stories. This is true. But I'd rather learn lessons from other people's stories than from my own ignorant decisions, thank you. Story lessons are cheaper and less painful than the Hard Knocks School.

I made plenty of bad decisions when I started my business. I've had my share of hard knocks. I share some of my story and the lessons I've learned in the pages that follow. My story gives you the option to avoid some of the dumb mistakes I made. You will, of course, make your own dumb mistakes. I'm sure there were a few I missed.

An introduction should give you some context to the rest of the book. So there are a few things I need to say up front.

Imagine I'm sitting across the table from you, nothing formal. We're sharing coffee (or your beverage of choice). I'm unraveling all the lessons I've learned from 20 years of running a service business out of my home.

You will find that I have strong opinions. The lessons I learned from bad decisions are burned deep in my soul. I'm animated and passionate when I talk face-to-face. I often neglect my coffee that's cooling on the table.

Strong opinions sometimes translate to "bossy." Since you're not actually sitting across the table I can't hear you reply to me, "You're full of crap." But I've tried to imagine those times you'll respond with similar comments. I've included your imagined responses in some places. (Yes, I realize I'm putting words in your mouth.)

I'm not so arrogant to claim that this book contains everything you need to be a successful entrepreneur. Read a ton of books before you make that leap. Better to know more than you need than to need more than you know.

I want you to get a head start I didn't get as an entrepreneur. I want you to see that you need more than merely the right skills and tools. Becoming an entrepreneur is as much about mindset as talent and skills: a fact I didn't discover until I had many years in business under my belt.

You can break your addiction to your paycheck. But you have to learn to quit thinking like an employee and start thinking like an entrepreneur. You won't learn this with a checklist. I don't have a ten-step program. You develop the mind of an entrepreneur by doing. I'll point the way. But you'll have to decide to take the first step to really start your own business and leave your paycheck behind.

Chapter 1

The Start of Addiction

"The three most harmful addictions are heroin, carbohydrates, and a monthly salary." — Nassim Nicholas Taleb

You've been trained all of your life to be an employee. Adults ask, "What do you want to be when you grow up?" almost as soon as you leave behind training diapers. I'm betting that "entrepreneur" wasn't on your list of answers. What four-year-old can even pronounce the word? And fire fighters or dancers are much easier jobs for a child to imagine.

At some point in your childhood, you realized your parents worked at jobs to get money. And you connected the dots to see it took money to buy the toys or candy you craved. "It costs too much," they would tell you. You knew the higher the cost, the more begging and pleading it took to get your parents to relent and cough up the money.

You never considered you might have to do something miserable and boring to earn money. And as you grew up, your list of fun-sounding jobs expanded. Your "future career" probably changed daily, depending on your mood.

Your indoctrination into the collective of the employed began in earnest when you started school. Modern education is designed to mold you into a good employee. You learn how to follow instructions, take your turn and get along with others, all of which are good life skills to have. Who'd want to live in a place where everyone did whatever they wanted and to hell with everyone else?

But there's a fiendish purpose behind your scholarly socialization. Your future employer requires these skills. Good employees have to follow instructions, obey the rules and get along with others. You don't even realize it. Your education is designed to make you think like an employee.

Formal education teaches you how to gather information, assimilate it and repeat it back to your teachers, in the way they expect it to be presented.

You're judged by how well you remember the correct *standardized* answers. And the better you can remember stuff, the more rewards and kudos you get.

A-students are both revered and hated. They're the examples, the students you're supposed to be like. Your teachers say you should be creative and think critically. But they don't really mean it. You can only go so far down that road. Don't roam too far off the path with crazy notions or unrealistic dreams.

Hierarchy of Jobs

Somewhere in all your learning you discover the "Hierarchy of All Possible Jobs." Your teachers now tell you that your ability to remember your academic lessons will determine your place in this job pecking order. Janitor and trash collector are usually near the bottom. Doctor and lawyer are near the top. (Feel free to insert a lawyer joke here.)

You see your favorites from childhood on this master list too. But you've got the PWM — that's "people who matter" — in your life telling you your childhood dream job isn't really what you want to do. *You need to face reality and get a good job with benefits*, they say. *Get a job that pays you lots of money and then have fun when you're old and retired. The jobs you thought would be fun to do as a child aren't really going to get you where you want to be in life.*

So everyone tells you to study hard and apply yourself so you can grow up and be a success; in other words, get a good job. And it's not just coming from your teachers. Slack off in school and the PWM will say, *You better get your act together and study hard or you're going to be a big fat loser.*

Now, let me take a step back here and give credit to most of your teachers. It's not like they're doing these bad things to you on purpose. They're just trying to do their job (for the most part). They're convinced their lessons will make you a successful, productive member of society. But remember this: they are employees themselves. They're sold out to a system designed to create good employees. Your teachers want you to be a success, but "success" means you'll be an employee of some sort at the end of it all.

Risky Behavior

Your teachers may have told you about entrepreneurs. But they seemed like whacky risk-takers you really don't want to be associated with. Why would you risk your future on something crazy like starting your own business?

Being a doctor or a fireman were simple jobs to understand when you were a kid. Your education showed you the complexities as well as the relative risks and rewards within the Hierarchy of Jobs. But I'm guessing *entrepreneur* was still outside the boundaries of the list. So your education made being a trash collector seem like a safer alternative than being an entrepreneur.

And "safer" is the operative word here. You see, your brain is wired to avoid risk. Being an employee seems like the logical choice because it seems like a safe bet. You find someone to hire you and, as long as you produce the results they want, you've got a steady paycheck. You don't feel the risk like you would when you start a business. If you become an entrepreneur, your business could fail and you'd lose both your money and your job. That's risky. And losing something looks twice as big and scary to you as any good thing that might come to you.

Imagine I walk up to you on the street and offer you a wager on a coin flip. You pay me $1.00 for heads and I pay you $1.25 for tails. Do you take that bet? Now, you might be one of the few who will jump on these odds. Logic should tell you that a 50-50 chance that pays 25% is a great deal. But most people won't take that bet until the payoff is double: $2.00 gained if you risk $1.00.

You see, your brain is wired to fear loss. Twenty-five percent reward feels risky. You won't take the risk until the reward *feels* certain.

Your Lizard Brain

The part of your brain responsible for you feeling the fear of loss is called the amygdala by the scientists who study such things and invent names. But "lizard brain" is the common term used. The lizard brain controls your response to fear, hunger and sex. It shoots adrenaline into your body when you're in danger.

Say you're crossing the street and a truck is about to run you over. You don't want your logical brain in charge. You'll be squashed, as your logic says, "I perceive a truck coming toward me at great speed." Your lizard brain says, "Truck. DANGER!" and you turn into a world-class long jumper. Your lizard brain comes in handy when you need to act fast.

Your lizard brain also makes you afraid of potential danger and risk. Think about how you feel when your friend invites you to go skydiving this weekend. Do you feel fear? Do you hear your lizard brain ask, *Why would you jump out of a perfectly good airplane?* The default setting for the lizard brain is *fear.* In fact, it's lusting for the next fear-inducing situation. So even when you feel safe and content, your lizard brain is pacing the floor, anticipating the next crisis so it can spring into action.

You see, your lizard brain isn't rational. It doesn't make logical evaluations about fear. It's just afraid.

I'm sure you know people who have irrational fears. Of course, your own fears seem totally justified. Your lizard brain convinces your logical brain you are normal. It's other people who are afraid of silly things.

I knew a guy who was terrified of squirrels. He knew his fear wasn't logical, but he couldn't help the fact that squirrels terrified him. His wife likes to tell of the time she put a fake squirrel behind the toilet. They almost had to replace the bathroom door because he ran away so fast.

You may laugh like I did when I heard the story. But remember, you've got fears like this too — fears you know aren't logical. But you're afraid anyway. Read through a list of phobias. Surely you'll find one you identify with.

A Little Dash of Risk

On the other hand, you've learned to tell your lizard brain to be quiet about some of the things you do. Most of us need the thrill of risk and danger, in controlled doses. Roller coasters and horror flicks are good examples. The "danger" is under control enough to keep our lizard brain quiet, but you feel enough risk to make it feel fun.

The thing is, everyone has a different tolerance for risk. Some people free-climb sheer rock cliffs thousands of feet tall. Others won't climb a 10-foot ladder. Some people jump out of airplanes with a backpack full of nylon fabric and chords. And others never fly in an airplane, even though statistics prove you're more likely to die in a car wreck on the way to the airport. Similarly, you have a line of risk you won't cross. For most people, being a self-employed entrepreneur is on the other side of that line.

So it's your lizard brain telling you to be safe and choose a career from the Hierarchy of Jobs list. If you're lucky, your rational brain and your lizard brain negotiate a truce. You find a job with a balance between safety and excitement, a job that challenges and stretches you but still feels *safe*.

But you might not be lucky. Your lizard brain might seize your decision. So you take a job that feels rock solid. It's almost too safe: you've got no real stimulation or excitement. You dream of what could have been had you chosen differently, and you end up miserable. But now you're stuck, because you've got obligations, debts, and commitments that your "safe" job covers for you.

Handcuffed by Safety

When you're firmly entrenched in a "secure" job, your lizard brain will howl in protest if you ever have serious thoughts about doing something risky like starting your own business. The education that makes you a good employee, plus the voices of the PWM, conspires with your lizard brain to obliterate any thoughts of being an Entrepreneur.

Your job routine is like your school routine. You show up on time. You do the things they ask. You turn in your assignments on time. And the better you handle these assignments, the more you get rewarded, especially with money and promotions. So your lizard brain is happy because it feels safe. Your monthly salary satisfies your inner lizard.

But he doesn't get fat and lazy. Feeding that lizard just makes him bigger and stronger. Your routine becomes familiar. You make obligations and commitments. You take on debt and you buy stuff to make your life as comfortable as possible. And the more stuff you have, the stronger your inner lizard gets.

At this point, your paycheck addiction is complete. Any thought of losing the good stuff you've got makes your inner lizard scream in terror. At this point, even a fantastic, mind-blowing opportunity won't tempt you to leave your comfort zone. "You can't risk losing all this," whispers your inner lizard. "There's no guarantee you'll succeed if you do that!" You stay in your comfort zone. Your lizard brain links *familiar* to *safe*.

The common belief is that 60 - 80% of Americans hate their job. It's because of your lizard brain. You stay in a job you hate because the fear of leaving is bigger than the loathing you feel where you are. The devil you know is less scary than the devil you don't.

So, on one hand, your lizard brain makes it likely to choose some "safe" career path other than being an entrepreneur. On the other hand, it's highly unlikely you'll leave a job — even a crappy job — to become an entrepreneur. Your addiction to a regular paycheck is too strong. Your lizard brain screams like a siren at the mere thought. Starting a business feels like jumping out of a perfectly good airplane.

Motivation to Jump

What this means is you usually won't become an entrepreneur unless you're forced into it. Either your job sucks so badly that you get fed up and can't take it anymore . . . or you lose your job: you're fired or downsized. Or it could be something else. But it's unlikely you're going to wake up one morning and decide, "I'm going to become an entrepreneur." No addict changes his or her behavior until the pain of the addiction is greater than the fear of change.

When you finally say, *Enough! I'm sick of this!*, you'll take action to break your addiction and make some real changes. It doesn't matter whether it's drugs, unhealthy food, relationships or a job. When it gets bad enough — when you get fed up with all the crap — you reach the tipping point. Once you get there, you pull out the number for the rehab clinic, or the gym, or a lawyer or you read the books you bought the last time you had the crazy thought about becoming an entrepreneur.

Chapter 2

Think Like an Owner

So now you see how you've been conditioned to think and act like an employee. You stand in line, color inside the lines, follow instructions, give the right answers, do the work you're given. Your employer wants you trained well so you will be one of the cogs — and we wouldn't want the cogs in the machine to be getting their own ideas now, would we? Freethinking cogs foul up the work and crash the whole system.

As an entrepreneur, you'll have to unlearn a lot of the stuff you've been taught: all those lessons on how to behave and think like an employee.

And don't think advanced job training makes you any different. Your employer may offer continuing education or help you get an MBA. The intent of MBA programs, so I'm told, is to deprogram employees and teach them to think like managers. You see, managers must think differently than regular employees. They make management-type decisions. And, yes, they have to live with the results of their decisions.

But being a manager of a business isn't the same thing as being the owner. Your own butt is on the line when you are the owner. And you'll get a whole new understanding of the phrase "lose your butt" if you make wrong decisions.

Now you're probably thinking I'm going to give you an outline of everything you need to know to be a successful entrepreneur. So let me get the disappointing news over with before we go much further. Yes, you can take the information I'm giving you here and go start your own business. But no book contains everything you need to know. And a book with everything you need to know to be an entrepreneur would intimidate the hell out of you. You'd be too overwhelmed to take the first step. So I'm merely giving you a significant head start I didn't have.

Unconscious Ignorance

I didn't even know my mind wasn't right when I started in business. I didn't know anything at all about running a business. Some have said that entrepreneurs have two main characteristics: courage and ignorance.

That was me. I had unconscious ignorance. I didn't know how many things I didn't know.

I was unaware that my mind wasn't right. I didn't know I'd been steeped in the culture of the employee mentality. It didn't even occur to me that I might have to think differently to be an entrepreneur. I just decided to go out and start my business. Yes, I was in business, but I had the mindset of an employee. The results were disastrous.

Changing Your Mind

Entrepreneurs think differently. And to move from being an employee to being an entrepreneur, you'll have to learn to think differently too. But I'm not going to give you a 10-step system. There's no list of entrepreneur thoughts you can do or learn, checking them off as you go.

So even though I'm giving you four examples of how you have to think differently as an entrepreneur I want to be clear this isn't a list. You see, you check items off of a list. Checking them off means you're finished. None of the things you learn as an entrepreneur are truly finished. There's always more to learn. You can always be a little better.

Also, these four examples of entrepreneur thinking are not an exhaustive list. They're merely illustrations.

They are the areas I noticed the biggest shift in my own thinking. Once you learn to think like an entrepreneur you'll find scores of ways you differ from your old way of thinking as an employee.

Thinking Like an Entrepreneur

1. You are it.

Anything that gets done in your business begins with you and ends with you. You will make each and every decision down to the gnat's derrière details. And every decision you make will impact your business. Every decision affects the amount of money you bring home (or maybe the money you could lose).

You may have dreamed of a time when your boss wasn't constantly telling you what to do. Well, this is it. You are your own boss when you're an entrepreneur. Your boss won't step through the door and tell you what to do next.

And you will be surprised how scary it feels. You may have hated your boss always telling you what to do. But you at least had some cover if something went sideways. Your boss' bad decision didn't land totally on you. As an entrepreneur, you make every decision and live with the consequences. It's like walking a high wire without a net.

Now, you may be comfortable making decisions. You might be good at making decisions. If so, you're in the minority. Decisions are hard for most people. So for those of us in the room who aren't so good at making decisions, here's my advice: practice. Practice making decisions even if you're already good at it.

So you may be feeling like Dorothy when she meets the Wizard of Oz and says, "That's it?" *Practice making decisions* is your great advice? Perhaps you were expecting something more profound.

But it really is that simple. Making small decisions with confidence and certainty helps you make the big ones with the same feeling of confidence. Certainty *feels* harder with big decisions. You never seem to have as much information as you'd like. But that's just part of the hand you're dealt. And big decisions feel different because the outcome is more important. But we were talking about practicing on small decisions.

What's For Lunch?

Tell me if you've ever been in this scenario. You're with a group of friends and it's time for lunch. Someone says, "Where do you want to go for lunch?" You usually get a lot of "humminah, humminah" from the group because no one wants to stick his or her neck out and make a decision.

So here's where you can start practicing. Next time you're in this situation, make a decision and put it out there. Don't you usually say, "I don't care. Where do you want to go?" Well, cut it out. Make a decision and speak up.

Sure, someone will say, "I'm allergic, I don't like, I'm not in the mood for . . . ." So make another decision. If you're practicing you should be presenting places to eat without all the dithering around that usually happens for such a simple decision.

Keep practicing when you get to the restaurant. Look at the menu. Read the descriptions. Decide quickly. Fold up the menu and put it down. Don't sit at the table and wonder if you really want something else.

Get in the habit of getting the information you need from the menu and deciding. What's the worst that can happen? The item you didn't order was the chef's specialty? So you miss out and get a so-so meal. Learn from it and make a better decision next time.

Keep finding ways to practice your decision-making. Find other small decisions you have to make during your day. Make them on purpose and with conviction. Don't second-guess yourself once you've made your decision. Decide, and then live with the outcome. Remember, you're practicing.

Decisions are difficult because deciding is like making a cut. There is no back arrow, restore function. When you decide you need a board 72 inches long, you draw a line and saw it off. If you later discover you need it 73 inches, it's too late. The cut is made. Likewise, if you order lasagna at lunch it's too late to change your order when a steaming pizza is delivered two tables over. Your order is in the system and you can't change it now.

You see, decisions feel difficult for you because you cut off all your other options once you decide. You're stuck with your choice. So you eat the lasagna when it comes and forget about the pizza.

You Own the Decision

It's frightening. You have the rewards and failures of all your decisions as an entrepreneur. You're responsible. No matter how much you want to, you can't pass off the decision-making responsibility to someone else. So identify areas where you waffle and dither. Develop some guts in these areas. Make those decisions with purpose and conviction. Because you can't decide not to decide. No, you won't always make the best decision or even the right decision . . . which brings me to the next point.

Failure is an Option

2. You must learn to fail.

Your boss and employer expects you to make the right decision every time. It's your job to be right. If you screw up, you get a hand-slap. If you major-ly screw up, you get fired. If you royally screw up, you get fired and then blackballed so no one else wants to risk hiring you. You've got a huge incentive to avoid screwing up when you're an employee.

You only make "safe" decisions when you're in a meat grinder like this. You base your decisions on keeping your job and covering your butt. And it doesn't matter how low or high up on the food chain you are, whether you're in the highest levels of management or you're the mail clerk. You follow protocol and procedures when you're an employee. You don't risk failure.

If you decide to hire employees in your business, you're going to expect the same thing from them: to follow your company policy and avoid mistakes. Employees who fail should lose their jobs because it's their job to do things right.

Your perspective as the owner has to be the opposite. You're going to make wrong decisions. You're going to make decisions that fail. You're going to make decisions that fail and cost you money. That's the essence of your job as an entrepreneur. Not that you try to make bad decisions or try to fail on purpose. But you can't play it safe. You have to try new things. And you have to learn quickly from failures and flops.

Imagine walking through the inside of a maze. You pick a direction and hit a dead end. You turn around and try a different way. And you've got to remember not to walk down that dead-end path again. This is the life of an entrepreneur. You make decisions and try things without any guarantee they will be right. And you'll go down some dead-ends before you find the path that works for you.

Failure is Good

You've been trained to avoid failure. It was unacceptable. It meant you were a loser. It was a step on the path to ruin. You never wanted to see one of your school papers handed back bleeding red ink with a big fat F.

Your lizard brain interprets failure as pain, suffering, danger and death. "Don't do that! We'll die," your lizard brain screams. So this natural inner fear of failure conspires with the conditioning you got from school and society, telling you not to take risks because you don't want to fail.

If you grew up in the last couple of decades, our enlightened American society saved you from the pain of failure for a while. Kids' sports teams now give "participation awards" where everyone gets a trophy — no one loses and no one wins. We don't want little Johnny or little Mary to feel like a failure.

But then, a few years later, Johnny and Mary are thrown into competitive sports where there's no glory for second place. We only celebrate the winners. They get the trophies and the fame. Second place is just the closest loser.

So you learn to fear failure. You learn failure must be avoided at all costs. You don't learn to embrace failure as a way to learn and improve your game. No, you're just a loser when you fail.

Playing to Win

Your fear of failure means you end up playing the game of life trying to "not lose." Playing any game to "not lose" means you plan your strategy on safe bets. You only take calculated risks. You want wide margins.

Watch any sporting competition and see what happens when one side has a big lead. The other team or competitor often makes a comeback. The team or person playing to win has a good chance to beat a team or person playing to "not lose." Playing a game, any game, to "not lose" is a good way to fail.

Yes, you risk failure when you play to win. But playing to win is also the best way to keep from losing. You think differently when you play to win. Playing to win means you take risks, you take chances. You keep pushing the borders. You test your limits. You do more than you thought you ever could. You're trying to win; you're not trying to just maintain an advantage.

Think about what winning teams do when they lose. Winning teams don't agonize over mistakes. Instead, they learn from mistakes. They accept the mistakes, work to correct them and move on. No, they don't overhaul their game plan after a loss. Winners stay focused on the fundamentals of the game, because they know it's the fundamentals that make them win. Losing merely reveals a weakness in their skill in executing the fundamentals of the game.

Execute the Fundamentals

Remember the first fundamental of entrepreneurship is decision making. I would go so far as to say it is *the* fundamental. And I'll remind you again that you have full responsibility for every decision.

Pay attention here. You must accept the fact that you're going to make a wrong decision. Sometimes you're going to fail. Learn to fail well. Consider this axiom:

Wisdom is the ability to make good decisions. Wisdom comes through experience. Experience is the result of making bad decisions.

Fail Well

So what does it look like to fail well? Here are a couple of suggestions.

First of all, call it failure as soon as possible. You usually have some early indications when your plans are heading south. Do what you can to fix the problems and head off disaster. But don't double down on a losing hand if you've made a bad decision. Remember, your lizard brain is going to be screaming at you when things start to fall apart: *You don't want to lose this!*

Your inner lizard will feed you crazy schemes to keep you "safe," to keep you from failing. But you need your rational brain to step in now and take an honest look at the situation. And, yes, failure is an option. Sometimes it's your best option.

Once you've identified failure, the second part is to accept it. Cut your losses. Salvage what you can and move on. Don't try to snatch success from the jaws of defeat. The jaws of defeat have sharp teeth. You're likely to be mangled in the process.

These two lessons — making decisions and admitting failure — cost me thousands of dollars to learn.

Losing Big in Real Estate

I bought a house in 2005, planning to fix it up and flip it to a new owner. I dreamed of what I'd do with a nice, fat profit. There were no *Flip this House* shows on HGTV yet. But, even so, there were a lot of other people trying to buy and flip houses. So good deals were hard to find. Bu've only invested a few hundred dollars rather than thousands. But the principle is the same no matter what new thing you might try. Identify failure early, accept it, learn from it and move on.

Failure Is Not Perpetual

Don't get me wrong. You can't fail all the time. You've still got to strive for success. But you must understand, failure is part of being an entrepreneur. One of the most famous quotes about failure comes from Thomas Edison. He supposedly said, "I've not failed. I now know over 1,000 ways not to build a light bulb." He also said, "I make more mistakes than anyone else I know. And sooner or later I patent most of them."

So, yes, failure is part of being an entrepreneur. But when you're an entrepreneur you never see failure as the end. Failure means you're just getting started. You've got to keep pushing your boundaries and trying new things until you succeed.

3. Learn to Love Your Profit

You have skills. You have abilities. When you're an employee, you find someone who'll give you money for your skills. And you used your skills to make money for your employer. And, when you're an employee, your employer has to pay you less than you're worth. Your employer can't pay you the market value of your skills because he will go broke if he does. Business owners have to make a profit.

You were paid a salary or by the hour as an employee. As a business owner, you have to think about profit. There's an emotional and psychological difference between salary and profit. You have to understand the emotions and psychology of profit when you're an entrepreneur.

When you work as an employee, your employer has to sell enough stuff to cover the expenses of the business as well as make a profit. Your salary is an expense to the business. The profit from the business, after you and everyone else get paid, is what the owner of the business uses to feed his family. You have to produce profit for the company when you're an employee. If there's no profit, the business goes broke.

So your employer can't pay you what you're worth. He has to make a profit.

Profit and Twinkies

You may remember what happened to the Hostess company. Hostess was struggling to survive because the economy went south at the same time people started cutting back on carbohydrates. And gluten became the latest "devil ingredient" that was going to kill us all, further depressing sales.

The company owners said they couldn't afford to pay the wages the employees' union demanded. The employees didn't believe them and went on strike. The owners decided they couldn't be profitable anymore and closed the company. So instead of getting the money they demanded, the employees lost their jobs.

Howls of protest came from the media and the general public. How could the owners be so hard-hearted and put all those employees out of work? The outrage was based on the fact that most people are employees and they think like employees.

The Hostess workers and the general public forgot that it's the profit from the business they work for that pays their wages. What incentive do the business owners have to risk their money and invest blood, sweat and tears to keep a business running and not get a profit?

Think about it this way. Would you work at your job as an employee for no pay? Would you pay money to work at a job with a promise from your employer that you might get paid sometime in the future? Probably not. But that's what an entrepreneur does.

An entrepreneur invests money and spends time to create a business, all in hopes that the business will someday make a profit. A business owner with no profit is working for free. And he may be spending his own money too, just to keep the business going.

As a business owner, you've got to prioritize profit. Profit, not wages, is what keeps your doors open. You make profit by selling your stuff. And, when you're selling services, you can't just look at what you were paid as a salary. Remember, wages are not profit. You'll have to charge more for your skills than any employer will pay.

Buy Low, Sell High

I confused wages with profits when I first started my handyman business. I charged an hourly rate based on the high end of carpenter's wages at the time. I couldn't figure out why I was going broke. I didn't charge enough to cover all the business expenses over and above what I considered.

Every employer buys an employee's skills at wholesale and sells them at retail. I had to realize I was selling my skills as a retail business. I wasn't just a guy working for a wage.

Think about it this way. When you go to the dentist, you aren't just paying for his or her time. You're paying for talent and experience. The dentist invests time, money and practice to hone his or her skills. The dentist's skill is a commodity you pay for. The money you pay is profit on the investment of time and money the dentist made to get those skills.

You have to see your talents and skills in the same way as an entrepreneur. The fact you've had a job means your skills, knowledge and experience are valuable enough for someone to pay you money.

You take those same skills to the marketplace as an entrepreneur. When you do, you'll have to charge retail prices for your skills. To do this, you'll have to quit thinking about salary and paychecks: stop that addiction. Start thinking in terms of profit for your business.

4. Holistic thinking

You might be able to do extra work as an employee and show "initiative." Some bosses like initiative.

Showing drive and moxie could earn you a promotion and more responsibilities.

But you don't have total freedom. You still have to work inside the lines. You have to stick to your job description. You can fudge the lines a bit, but for the most part you've got to answer to someone else.

And you're expected to just do your own job. Step out of bounds and your co-workers and your boss will come down on you. They'll tell you not to mess with work outside the scope of what you're paid to worry about.

As an entrepreneur, you have no lines. You're responsible for everything about your business. You are free to make your business anything you choose.

The Security of Boundaries

The idea of making your own rules sounds so good when you're having a bad day at work. You can pick your reason: stupid boss, no one appreciates you, lazy co-workers, the list goes on. But in reality, the "no boundaries" thing is rather uncomfortable. Even if you have a crappy job and a lunatic boss, you still have some security in your boundaries, in knowing what's expected. You feel secure because you've been trained all your life to color in the lines and follow the rules.

You won't realize the feeling of security these boundaries give you until those boundaries are suddenly gone. You feel like you're adrift on a wide ocean. When the realization hits you: *Crap! What do I do now?*

Now you get to (have to) make your own rules and all the decisions. When you're in the middle of it, you'll find the reality of no boundaries much scarier than you imagined.

As an entrepreneur, you have to make every decision at every level of your business. You'll feel as if you're setting out for Hawaii with only a rowboat and a compass: no map and no GPS.

You're probably good at your job as an employee. But what you do as an employee is only part of what running the company is all about. When you're an entrepreneur, you have the whole enchilada. And now you have to take care of everything: the stuff you do well and all the other things you're not so good at. You can't just do the things you're good at. You can't just do the work that's fun. You have to do everything.

The Easy Road

The easy path is to keep trudging off to the daily grind. Hang onto the security of a regular paycheck. You'll have the illusion of security. They'll keep paying you as long as you follow the rules and stay inside the lines. They'll tell you your mind is right as long as you conform.

But when you decide to become an entrepreneur, either by choice or by necessity, you'll have to break out of that mold and learn to think differently. Learning to think like a business owner takes time, experience and practice. Having the mind of an employee while trying to be an entrepreneur will bring you lots of grief and put you on the fast track to being out of business.

Take the Challenge

As an entrepreneur, you have to learn how to make decisions with conviction and confidence. You have to learn to think in terms of profit, not salary. You have to learn to fail and recover quickly. You have to learn how the whole business runs because you're it now — and the keyword here is *learn*.

You may already be feeling overwhelmed by all the stuff I'm throwing at you. That's normal. But keep in mind that lots of people start in business without even knowing they have to learn all of this. I certainly started that way. And some of these lessons you only learn "on the job" once you jump in and start your own business.

To succeed as an entrepreneur, you have to start learning and keep learning. And you'll lose your edge if you're not at least a little bit intimidated by the challenges you choose. So all of this may be overwhelming. But you can do it if you want it badly enough.

Chapter 3

Making Money

I started in business with no plan, no direction, no clue and a few carpentry skills. I'd been a do-it-yourself remodeler for years. My wife and I rehabbed two homes from foundation to roof. We'd just finished building a new home from the foundation up, with the help of family and friends. I had the truck. I had the tools. I had some general fix-it skills. So I said to myself, "Self, why not start a handyman business?"

Some decisions should have a warning label. Seemingly small decisions can turn your life upside down. Even big decisions, like getting married, can surprise you. You say, "I do," and you don't fully realize that you have to do and do if you want your marriage to work. Deciding to start in business was that kind of decision for me.

Talk about feeling adrift at sea. One day, I was just a guy. The next day, I'm in business . . . or so I thought. I wouldn't say I was an entrepreneur when I began. An entrepreneur has some clue of what he or she is doing. I was clueless. Sure, I was in business, but what to do now? My wife's advice didn't help. She was clueless too. So I did what little I knew.

People in business have cards. So I made up some business cards. I hit the streets to find some business. A few people hired me and I was off to the races, or so I thought.

I did good work. I took on anything and everything, even cleaning trash out of rental houses. I figured, "Hey, at least I'm making money."

Yes, money was coming in. And money went out too: for tools, supplies and expenses. I stayed busy. I worked hard. And I made $3,000 that year.

My wife kept asking why I made so little. I said, "I don't know. I'm working as much as I can."

I worked harder and longer my second year in business. And I raised my prices a tiny bit. But I didn't send any money in for my taxes. My wife had taxes taken out of her paycheck. She still had a "real" job. So I went on, fat, dumb and happy, thinking everything would be fine. The increase in business meant I owed $2,000 in taxes.

I hadn't planned ahead. I had no bookkeeping system. I had no idea if I made a profit. My year-end, required-by-the-IRS tax filing showed a profit. But I didn't feel as if I'd made money. As much money went out as what came in. At least, that's the way it seemed.

My wife still kept asking how come I worked so hard and made so little money. I was still clueless. But I decided I had better figure out the answer.

There was so much I didn't know about being self-employed it was scary. I was never much for planning. I remember a line from a movie that goes something like, "I'm a Marine. We don't plan. We improvise." I'd draw out detailed plans for my remodeling and construction projects. But making plans for my business? Not so much.

Plan Your Work: Work Your Plan?

Yeah Right . . .

I admire you people who set goals. You all seem to have your stuff together. You think ahead. I bet you've even got a draft of a business plan. You bought this book just to see if you left anything out. Don't worry. You left out plenty.

One of the reasons I'm not giving lists of stuff — you know, the top 10 ways to have a successful home-based business — is because there's always an 11th or 12th thing out there lurking around the corner.

Making lists is good. Planning is good. I've had to learn to do both. But sometimes you have to improvise. You have to look at things you've never done before and say, "Sure, I can do that." You have to jump in and start, then figure out the details along the way

And if you're the type who plans everything down to the gnat's derrière, you need to remember that nothing ever goes as planned. If you're a "free spirit," you have to learn how to plan. And if you're a planner you have to learn to improvise. Most importantly, you have to learn when it's time to plan your work and work your plan or when you've got to "pull off a MacGyver" and muddle through with a twisty-tie, duct tape and WD-40.

If you like the idea of a traditional business plan, by all means do it. I once attempted making a traditional business plan after I'd been in business a few years. I even bought a computer program. It was supposed to help. It just made my head spin. I gave up. It was futile.

I think the linear logic of a traditional business plan derailed me. I'm not a linear thinker. I don't start at the beginning and work my way through to the end. I'd rather start in the middle and work my way out to the edges. And when I have to come up with a linear, logical plan, I prefer to use graphics rather than a boring outline. My business plan looks more like this:

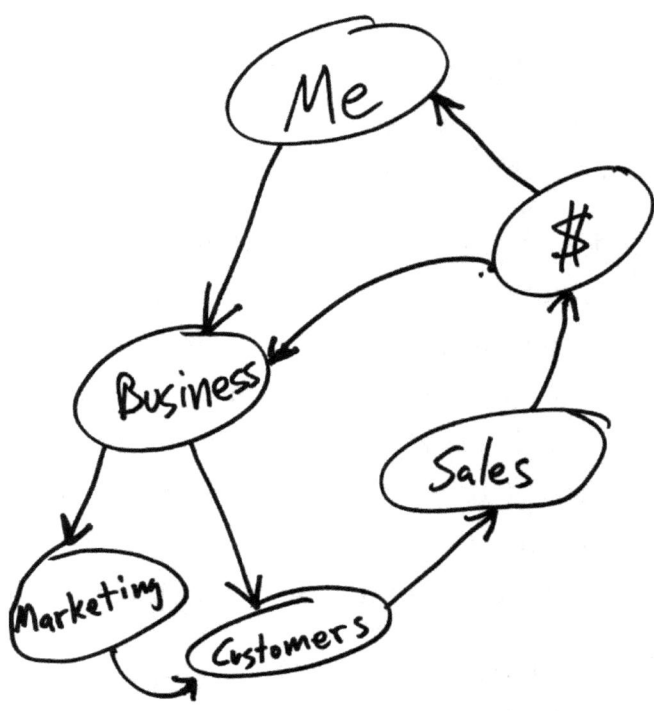

If you go looking for a loan to start your business, any investor will want to see your business plan. I can tell you now, they won't be impressed if bring in a plan like mine, sketched on a napkin. So do a traditional business plan for yourself if you're a list maker and planner. You might find it helpful to do a traditional business plan even if you're more of a sketch-it-on-a-napkin person.

Business gurus will say you need a business plan. And you can find lots of good resources online to help you write one if you choose to do so. Some of the gurus say you should spend several months gathering the information for your business plan. Like I said, a bank or investor will want this kind of research and a formal style of business plan.

But if you're going to bootstrap your business — invest all your own money — you won't have to make the typical business plan if you don't want to. Don't follow my example and just fly by the seat of your pants. I can tell you for sure you need some kind of a plan. The barebones minimum plan you should use is there in the napkin-sketch illustrated above.

But Wait! There's More

Sketching on a napkin is easy. But now you've got to take your sketch and get the information those circles identify. You see, my napkin sketch has some of the same points a traditional business plan has. It's just in a format I can understand and relate to. Yes, I know you linear thinkers believe I'm nuts.

Keep in mind that creating a business plan doesn't guarantee success. I'm sure you can name major businesses that made business plans and still failed. You've probably heard the old saying, "If you fail to plan, then you plan to fail." I always felt like the sinner in the back of church when I heard this. Like I said, my approach to life has been, "Why plan when you can just improvise?" This was just my excuse for not doing the hard work of making plans.

Yes, you can make careful plans and fail anyway, but making no plan at all is like playing the lottery. You may beat the odds, but I doubt it. So put your business plan in an outline if that's your process, or grab a stack of napkins and markers and let's start planning.

You, Your Business and Customers

I'm going to go out on a limb and suppose that you've got at least a fuzzy idea of a business you might start. I mean, you bought a book about starting a business, for heaven's sake. I'll make another safe bet. Your business idea is something you're passionate about. And if not passion, you at least have some talent for it.

Do you daydream about how much fun it will be? Yeah, to just do what you love all day long. Sit back for a moment and let your mind go there. *Ah, just imagine how great life will be.*

Okay, that's enough. Slap yourself back to reality. You've got a lot of work to do before you can get there for real.

Here's the first step to bring your idea to the marketplace. You've got to identify who your customers are. Get something to write on. Tell me who your ideal client or typical customer is. Describe a real person here. No abstract generalities. Remember, we're planning. Get your info on those napkins.

Now don't go and tell me, "Everyone needs what I've got." Even if that were true (which it's not), you can't sell to everyone. Some people won't care if they need what you're selling; they won't buy it at all. Some people will need what you've got and they'll buy it from someone else. Some people will ignore you completely. No, your ideal customer isn't *everyone.*

On top of all this, people don't decide to buy something just because they need it. They buy the things because they want them.

Niche Yourself

Like I said, you can't have "everyone" as your customer. Here's a secret: the more you narrow down your criteria for who your ideal customers are, the more successful you'll be.

Let's suppose, for example, you're going to offer window washing. Owners of tall office buildings need their windows washed. But if you're the new guy or gal and a small operation, these big building owners probably aren't your ideal customers.

You could decide to go after homeowners. But how do you let them know about your service? You'll have to spend money to advertise, spend time walking all over town posting flyers or knock on doors to try to make sales.

So you decide your best market is business storefronts owned by individuals: mom and pop stores. You can walk in and make your pitch directly to the decision-maker. Narrowing down your ideal customers like this is called a "niche market."

Do you see why I say you can't sell to "everyone?" Narrow down your business to find your niche market. Make a profile of your ideal customers. Are they single or married? How old are they? Where do they live? Where do they work?

If they are married, who makes the decision to hire you or buy your product: the husband or the wife? What is their income range? What is their education level? What triggers their buying decision for your product or service?

This kind of specific information gives you a target to focus your business. You're no longer aimlessly searching for just anyone to buy your product. You could even go so far as to name this fictitious ideal customer. Create a profile of his or her characteristics, answering the questions I just asked.

Once you've identified your niche, you're ready for the next step.

Marketing Your Business

You know what they say: you never get a second chance to make a first impression. The good impression your business creates on your potential, ideal customers will come from marketing. Marketing and money are the two most important parts of your business. Because they're important, I'll talk about them in more detail later.

But you have to make some money before you can worry about managing your money or planning your marketing. Making money means you've got to sell something.

Selling Your Time, Talents and Products - TT&P

You only have three things you can sell: your time, your talent or your products. You're familiar with selling your time and your talents as an employee. And you may have been involved in creating and/or selling products for your employer. So let's set talent and products aside for right now. Yes, I'm using TT&P to talk about what you sell, but let's just focus right now on selling your time.

I started in business by selling only my time. I charged my customers the going, hourly rate an employed carpenter made. I'd heard the term "overhead," but I had no clue what it was or that it applied to my business.

What I learned the hard way is that you have to charge enough for your TT&P to cover your overhead and still make a profit. Selling your time based on an employee's wages won't cut it. Every business charges more per hour than they pay their employees. Every business has overhead. And if you don't cover your overhead, you're on your way to being broke and out of business.

You can find plenty of businesses that operate by selling time. Attorneys operate on "billable" hours. Computer programmers, house cleaning, dog walking, plumbers, childcare . . . the list goes on. You pay an hourly rate for all kinds of services.

So, in your business, how do you decide what to charge? Your price per hour determines your profit and whether you live or die as an entrepreneur.

How Much Money Do You Need?

Your first step is to discover how much money you need. Then you can decide whether you can sell enough of your TT&P to your niche market at a profit.

So you first have to put together your personal budget. Take your monthly bills and convert them into an annual budget. This budget isn't for running your household; it's for planning the income you need from your business.

The following example is as if your business is your only source of income. Now, you may have a spouse or partner still working as an employee somewhere. If that's the case, you should use this same system, but calculate the money your salary contributes to your household income.

Here are some examples of expenses you'll have. Fill in any categories you might have that aren't listed here:

Personal budget:

- Tithe and/or charitable giving
- Retirement fund
- Savings fund
- Income taxes

Home expenses:

- Home mortgage or rent
- Insurance
- Real estate taxes
- Maintenance & repairs
- Home improvements

Utilities:

- Electric
- Gas
- Water
- Trash
- Phone and/or cell phone
- Cable/Internet

Food:

- Groceries
- Restaurants, pizza delivery etc.

Auto:

- Loan
- Fuel
- Maintenance/repairs
- Taxes
- Insurance

Medical:

- Doctors, dentists, chiropractor, etc.
- Health insurance
- Life insurance
- Gym membership

Miscellaneous:

- Gifts
- Clothing
- Hair care: stylists, barber, etc.
- Subscriptions and books
- Vacation/Travel
- Recreation, hobbies and leisure

Figure out everything you spend for the year. Be sure to include payments you make that don't happen every month. For example, your car registration is a once-a-year expense. Christmas and birthday gifts aren't monthly expenses. You get the idea.

Also, my list isn't all-inclusive. You'll have expenses that aren't here on my list. And some categories listed here won't apply to your household.

There are three categories listed above I want to emphasize.

Income tax: When you're an employee, you don't have to think about regular payments to the IRS. Your employer takes care of that for you. But you've got to pay the IRS yourself when you're self-employed. Don't forget you pay your Social Security and Medicare taxes too — twice. Your employer matched your Social Security and Medicare payments. Now, you pay as both the employer and the employee.

Tithe: It's a universal principle . . . givers gain. Giving is as much for your benefit as for those you give to. Make charitable giving a priority, and do it each month. Here's the secret to effective giving: don't give from what's leftover. You'll never have anything left to give if you give what's leftover. Give first. Then pay your bills. Trust me, it benefits you to be a giver.

Vacation: You have to pay yourself for it. Include both the money you spend on vacation and the money you'll need to pay your bills while you're gone. I'll talk more about taking time for yourself in chapter six. For now, just trust me. Put money for vacation time in your budget.

Money for Your Business

Now you need to put your business budget together. You are going to keep your business expenses separated from your personal expenses, aren't you? Open a bank account for your business. Business income goes in and business expenses come out. And that's it. It's your business account.

Now, if you're already using just your personal account for your business and personal expenses, put down this book and go open a business account. Yes, it's that important.

Keep your business money separate from your personal money. And don't buy personal stuff from your business account. Your business budget needs to reflect all the expenses you have to run your business.

Business Budget

- [ ] Payroll
- [ ] Liability insurance
- [ ] Bank fees
- [ ] Dues and memberships
- [ ] Subscriptions
- [ ] Marketing
- [ ] Business vehicles

Office:

- [ ] Supplies
- [ ] Equipment
- [ ] Software
- [ ] Postage
- [ ] Telephone

☐ Cell phone

☐ Internet

Miscellaneous:

☐ Professional fees

☐ Licensing fees

☐ Tools and equipment

☐ Travel

☐ Outside services/Contractors

☐ Bad debt

☐ Future equipment

☐ Personal development and professional continuing education

How You Get Paid

You might not know how much money to budget in some of these categories. And some of these categories won't apply to your business. You may also need additional categories not included in this list.

The important thing to note is that the total amount of your personal budget goes on line one of your business budget. "Payroll" is how you get paid. The money you need to make to cover your personal expenses has to come from the business.

I know, this point seems obvious, but this is one of those facts that can live in your head but not make it to your gut.

The thing is, we entrepreneurs tend to be creative types. So I can "know" all my money has to come from working in my business, but my gut gets influenced by unicorns and rainbows. Its easy to start acting like money is going to just magically appear from somewhere other than the line on my business budget labeled "payroll." But then again, this could be just me.

If you have employees, you'll have to include their salaries in this category as well. Along with employees' salaries, you'll need to add the employer contribution to social security, as well as any additional employee benefits you might offer. I'll talk more about employees in another chapter.

Important Stuff Worth Highlighting

There are a few categories about your business budget I want to point out and discuss in detail.

Vehicle: Think about whether you need a company vehicle? For a service business, and especially if you have employees, you may want the vehicles used in your business to be owned by your business. You can deduct actual expenses, as well as depreciation, for company vehicles.

On the other hand, the IRS will allow you to deduct mileage if you use your personal vehicle for business. You have to document business use, but if you're going to be a solo entrepreneur or a home-based business this mileage deduction might be better than the effort it takes to maintain records for a company vehicle.

I've used both methods in my business. I settled on using my personal vehicle and deducting the mileage. What's best for you? That's a question you should talk over with your accountant.

Liability insurance: You need business liability coverage. Your personal insurances don't usually cover you if you injure someone or damage something in the course of your business. Your type of liability coverage will depend on the kind of business you have. Are you working in customers homes or businesses? Or do customers come to a store or office to do business with you? Or you could have both. Prices and coverage vary. Spend time to find the best deal.

You've heard the stories of the crazy lawsuits some people bring. People will think you're no different than McDonald's or Wal-mart -- that you've got lots of money.

And they might think they can be the next lawsuit lottery winner if they trip on your doorstep.

Liability insurance won't prevent crazy people from trying to cash in on a big settlement. But it will protect you from the crazy person's attorney. Your insurance company will hire lawyers to settle the claim, not you.

Bad debt: I know you're a good person and you want to think everyone you meet is honest, like you are. You might be thinking, "I won't have any trouble with deadbeats."

But you'll have a few people who will try to rip you off. It's sad. They'll promise to pay but they won't pay, they'll give you a bad check, they'll dispute credit card charges. On the outside they'll seem like the most trustworthy people you'd ever hope to meet. Looks are deceiving. One of the companies that never did pay me was called "Integrity Construction."

Your experience with bad debt will depend on the business you create. It may be common practice for your type of business to have accounts receivable. Accounts receivable are customers you do work for and then send them a bill which they pay later.

You'll find a small percentage of people who won't pay at all if you decide to keep accounts receivable. And a lot of your accounts receivable customers will be slow to pay. For these, you'll have to devote time to pester and hound them. If you don't, your slow-paying customers can easily turn into non-paying customers.

I'll talk more about accounts receivable and ways you can get paid in a later chapter. Right now, however, you've got to allow a place in your budget for "bad debt." Yes, I know you're just guessing what that number might be and don't really want to think about deadbeats not paying you. Thinking about not getting paid is kind of a buzz-kill. But making your dreams happen means you'll face the realities of being in business without wavering.

Take a look at businesses similar to yours and do some digging to find out what kind of bad debt they experience. You might even be able to network with a similar business owner in another location — one you won't be competing against — who might be willing to share his or her experience with collections.

Meet Your Overhead

All of these expenses in your business budget create what's called your "overhead." Think of overhead like this: even if you have no sales or money coming in, you're going to have to pay overhead. Overhead is there all the time. And you have to sell enough of your TT&P with enough profit to meet and cover your overhead. We'll talk more about profit in a minute. But right now it's important for you to see your overhead is separate from your "job costs."

Job costs are expenses you have connected with selling your TT&P. For example, a house painter buys paint and puts it on the wall. A wedding photographer sells prints mounted in an album. A caterer buys food to cook for an event. The price of these materials are expenses related to doing the work, the job costs.

Here's the best way for you to understand the difference between job costs and overhead. You don't have job costs until you sell something, and these costs are directly tied to what you sell. But you'll have overhead costs whether you sell anything or not.

Another term for job costs is "Cost of Goods Sold" often abbreviated as COGS. COGS is a term used most often for businesses selling products. Service businesses typically refer to these expenses as *job costs*.

But COGS and job costs are essentially the same. These costs are directly tied to the TT&P you sell. If you're selling products your COGS is the wholesale cost as well as shipping. If you're selling your time, these costs are expenses related to each job you do: the supplies and materials you use in doing each job.

Now, if you want to be super-technical, you could divide the wages you pay to employees between overhead and COGS or job costs. Sometimes your employees are making you income: they're working for paying customers. And sometimes you carry them as overhead: they're just doing "filler" work and not bringing in money.

But the IRS instructions for Schedule C (one of the forms you use for business expenses) gives you a break. They read as follows: "Labor costs are usually an element of COGS only in a manufacturing or mining business. Small merchandisers (wholesalers, retailers, etc.) usually do not have labor costs that can properly be charged to COGS."

So if you need to hire employees right from the start, just figure their pay in "Payroll" and count it as part of overhead along with the money you need for your personal budget.

Once you have your personal budget and your business budget nailed down, you can see how much of your TT&P you've got to sell. This figure is your overhead. It's the money you need each year to break even.

In the next chapter we'll take these numbers and plug them into a formula so you can determine how much you have to charge for your TT&P. So pour yourself another cup of coffee and let's get down to the nuts and bolts of making profit in your business.

Chapter 4

Take Your Skills to Market

Did you freak out a little bit when you saw the size of your overhead? Thinking and dreaming about being in business is cool and fun. But it smacks you in the face when you put the number on paper: "I've got to sell a lot of stuff to make that much money."

Yes, it's intimidating. But pick your dreams back up off the floor. Let's break it down. You can't eat an elephant in one bite, but you can eat an elephant if you take one bite at a time.

This is reality. You have to charge enough for your TT&P to meet your overhead and give you a profit. I'll break it down at first as if you're selling only your time and talents. We'll talk about selling products later. The principle is the same. So pay attention and don't doze off here just because your business will only sell products.

Work Half-Days

You only get 24 hours in each day. You can't create more time, as much as you might want to. That's all. 24 hours each day . . . 168 hours a week, just like the rest of us.

Someone once said you can succeed in business by working half-days. Just pick which 12 hours of the day you want to work and get busy. The thing is, you can't keep the pace of 12-hour workdays long-term. Something in your life will break if you work that much: your health, your relationships, your sanity or all of the above. You don't want to be self-employed and end up working for a maniac.

You may still think of the standard workweek as 40 hours. I know this standard has changed in the last decade. Some people work crazy, long hours to keep their employers happy. But you'll find it difficult to bill customers for 40 hours of your time each week and still run your business.

You're going to have a lot of work to do in your business you can't bill your customers for. Doing estimates, meeting prospective customers, marketing, sales, filling out forms for the government, office work and accounting. You'll likely spend as much time on this "administrative" work as you do getting stuff done you actually get paid for.

You have to do the work of managing your business. No doubt. But you also need to work the hours you bill your customers for and bring in money. In my experience, trying to manage 40 "billable hours" a week is hard to keep up with. I've found a good standard is to use 30 hours a week (billable hours) working "in the field."

If you can keep up the pace to bill more hours than that, good for you. If you want to work more or less, just plug in the hours you choose to work *in the field* into the formula below.

The formula to find out what to charge for your TT&P is straightforward. What we'll do is compute the time you are going to have as "billable hours" compared to the money you need to cover your overhead.

A Calculator Might be Helpful Here

None of the following calculations are difficult. But you do need to understand the formula I describe here. Grab a calculator and punch in the numbers below as we go through. Ok, you can skip the calculator if you're a number wizard. The rest of us have to work harder. Put the numbers in your calculator to see for yourself how the formula works. Okay? Here we go:

Let's say your business budget is $80,000.00.

Divide by 52 weeks in the year: $1,539.46.

Divide this by 30 billable hours $52.00.

So you have to bill $52 per hour for your service, not counting job costs, in order to meet your overhead. The amount of money you need to cover your overhead is called "break even." Break even is the bare minimum amount of money you've got to have coming in to survive.

Selling Products

The formula works with products too. You will need to know how much profit you make on each item you sell. Then, you have to sell enough of your product so the profit covers your overhead.

Remember, your COGS aren't part of your overhead. Figure out your profit by taking your sales price and subtracting your COGS. And for the planning we're doing here, it's a good idea to break it all the way down to each individual item you sell.

Say you're selling cupcakes. And let's say you make $3 profit on each one you sell. Remember, profit is sale price less COGS. If you sell cupcakes for $4 and your COGS is $1, this will bring you $3 profit on each cupcake.

Put your profit into the formula above.

Weekly business budget: $1539.46.

Divide by $3 profit: 513.

If you sell 513 cupcakes each week of the year, you're breaking even in your business.

Wait a Minute!

You're probably paying close attention here. You wag your finger at me and say, "This formula is for working 52 weeks a year, without any breaks. Don't I get a vacation?"

You have a good point. So here's what you do. Figure how many weeks of the year you want to work — that is, doing work that brings in money — and use that number. Let's say you'll take two weeks as vacation.

Total business budget: $80,000.00.

Divide by 50 weeks: $1,600.00.

Divide by 30 hours: $54.00.

Using these figures, you'll have to bill $54 per hour for 30 hours each week you choose to work. Or, for selling products, you have to sell 533 cupcakes per week.

These figures show your "break-even" point: how much you have to sell to cover your overhead. Remember, you have to cover your overhead to keep yourself and your business afloat.

The Best Laid Plans Go Awry

So far, I've talked about your entire budget and sales numbers as if your business is going to go off like a rocket and just keep climbing. I hope that's the case for you. But you'll find that being self-employed is more like being on a roller coaster. You will have times your sales are up, and you'll have times when they dip.

Sheer drops are exciting and cool on roller coasters, but not so much fun in your small business. Hopefully your business won't have sheer drops, but you will have ups and downs.

You need to take the dips into account when you price your TT&P. You may not sell enough cupcakes each week. Your scheduled job may cancel or postpone. Stuff happens, and you have a week of no sales or fewer sales than you expect. Maybe you get sick or your equipment breaks. Stuff happens.

Your prices need to compensate for these contingencies so you don't fall short. Instead of working 50 weeks out of the year (that's deducting two weeks for your vacation), base your prices on a 45-week year. Yes, sometimes your plans go sideways, and you need to plan your budget so that a few bad weeks don't sink you.

You can take this basic formula and adapt it to find your break-even point for almost any business. But you'll need to do more than break even.

Don't Run a Non-Profit

You can't survive in business long-term if you're only breaking even. You have a job rather than a business if you're only breaking even. Granted, it's a job you've created. It's a job where you're the boss. But it's still just a job.

You have to generate profit if your business is going to survive. At the very least, you should figure in a net profit of 10% above your break-even point. Net profit is money left over after everything is paid.

This means that after you pay your job costs and cover your overhead (remember, this includes your personal budget and your income taxes) the money left is your net profit. It's money you can spend however you want.

You can go on vacation, buy a boat, buy a new car or you can reinvest it in your business. I've got some suggestions on what to do with your net profits in a later chapter. For now, let's just assume you're going to build in a 10% net profit. Using the numbers above, it will look something like this.

Break even budget: $80,000.00.

Divide by 0.9: $88,888.88.

Divide by 50 weeks: $1,777.77.

Divide by 30 hours: $60.00.

More Math Stuff

Now, you may wonder why you should divide by a decimal rather than just add 10% of $80,000. There is a difference between profit and markup. And this difference is especially important if you're selling merchandise. Here's a mathematical representation of the method I just described: Overhead / (1 - X% profit). So if you want a 10% net profit, you subtract the 10%

from 1 and use that decimal result as a divisor for your overhead.

Or, if you're like me, and like it explained as simply as possible: you turn the percentage of net profit you want into a decimal. You then subtract it from the number 1. You take the decimal you get after this subtraction and use it to divide your break-even number. (When you divide by a decimal, you get a bigger number.)

Ok, that still sounds pretty complicated. So here's how I do it.

To get a 10% net profit, subtract 0.1 from 1. The result is a 0.9 divisor (divisor is math-speak for what you use to divide your break-even budget by). A 15% net profit will be 1 - 0.15: a 0.85 divisor, and so on.

Are your eyes glazed over yet? Hey, I almost failed math in school. If I can figure this stuff out, anyone can. Take some time to go over it again if all this is new to you.

Bigger Margins on Products

Selling products at retail or selling a mix of services and merchandise means you need to pay closer attention to your profit margins. Your hourly rate calculations cover your overhead when you sell your time and talents. You add your profit afterward.

Your profit margin has to cover overhead *and* net profit when you're only selling products. You can easily slip below your break-even if your profit margin is too low. So understanding the difference between mark-up and profit is critical when you sell products alone or a mix of products and service.

Say, for example, you're going to sell food. This can cover a lot of possibilities, from a full-blown restaurant to catering to making wedding cakes, to name a few. The standard markup on food for most restaurants is 250-300%. You may think this is a lot. But this kind of markup will give you a gross profit of between 60 and 67%.

You might be able to keep a 10% net profit out of this gross profit if you're careful with your overhead.

Take, for example, a meal that sells for $25. Here's the breakdown.

Meal price: $25.00.

60% gross profit: $15.00.

Food cost: $10.00.

10% net profit: $2.50.

Your $10 food cost is COGS. It's marked up 250% to get your selling price.

All of your overhead will have to come from your 60% gross profit.

Your net profit of 10% is what remains.

Do Your Own Calculations

Take a few minutes to digest the figures above. You should be able to see how any increase in your overhead will immediately cut your net profit.

It's important you do your own analysis for how much to charge for your TT&P. Don't rely on industry standards to figure out how much to charge. Make your budgets and compute your overhead. Know how much you have to sell and at what price. And take some time to understand the difference between markup and profit.

Look at Your Competition

Here's where we get down to the nitty-gritty. Now, take a look at your competition. What businesses already sell your service or product? What do you know about them? Can you compete? How much do they charge?

If customers have a choice, do they have a good reason to choose you instead of your competition? Will your customers see any difference between you and your competition? Will they see you as better? Will customers be willing to pay a premium price for your TT&P if they think you're better?

Keep in mind there's a limit to how much your market will bear. You might produce the softest and best toilet paper, but you won't sell much if you price it at $20 a roll. It doesn't matter if it's as soft as a cloud and still strong enough to support a bowling ball. You won't have too many people willing to pay that price for toilet paper. Yes, some people will pay a premium for products and service . . . but there is still a limit to how much they'll pay.

I know it's hard to put yourself through this kind of reality check. Dreaming and hoping is a lot more fun. Why not just ignore your competition? Why risk seeing that you're not as good as you think you are?

Some American Idol hopefuls were funny because they're both clueless and inept. No one ever told them they weren't very good. But I'm like that sometimes. You are too. I think I'm wonderful. I think I'm great. And looking at what my competition is doing will burst my warm, fuzzy bubble. I don't really want cold, wet reality to smack me in the face. Give me my fantasy, thank you very much.

Dream On, Dream Until

Your Dream Comes True

Don't stop dreaming just because reality smacks you. Think about the hard work those talent show contestants put in. There's only one winner on the show. Even highly talented people are eliminated.

But you've also seen the runners-up be more successful than the winners. So look at your business competition as your panel of judges on a talent show.

Be bold and don't get yourself tied in knots because of fear. Find out everything you can about your competitors in your niche market. Believe me, your competition won't have the entire market sewn up. Look for the niche they're not serving and go after that piece of the market.

Lions, Tigers and Bears

The "Big Guys" are the easiest of your business competitors to find. The Big Guys are probably advertising, or they're at least known by word of mouth. You should already know who they are because you certainly wouldn't be thinking about starting a business doing something you know nothing about. You aren't, are you?

The Big Guys in your industry have an identity and a reputation. They're well established, and usually the prices they charge are at the top end of what your market will bear.

Your first task is to find out how much they charge for their TT&P. If you don't already know how much they charge, you can pose as a "secret shopper" and ask them. Now, take out your pricing plan and the budget you just completed. Do your figures line up with what the Big Guys are charging?

If your price is higher, you've got some hard choices to make. You've got to be very good at what you do to be the highest priced business in your market. And even if you're really that good, the Big Guys have years of a head start on you. Your odds aren't good when you're the new kid on the block and want to charge a premium price.

Don't scrap your business dream quite yet if your prices are higher. You can try to cut your expenses. Or you can narrow your market niche and find customers willing to pay a premium. The best solution is to do all of the above and modify what you offer in a way that sets your TT&P apart.

A Faux Example

Here's what I did to narrow my niche. My wife joined me in business once I became profitable. We expanded and offered "faux finishing" as well as handyman services. We dropped the handyman services a few years later. We specialized in only faux finishes.

Most people called us "painters." We got in the faux finishing niche before it exploded in popularity in the early 2000s. We had to explain how our talents were more artistic than your run-of-the-mill painter.

We'd get calls to paint a room: just roll flat paint on the wall. We always turned them down. Our niche was *faux painting*.

We charged a premium price for customers who recognized the difference between faux finishes and mere paint. Yes, we painted the walls like regular painters. But we didn't paint walls unless we also did the faux finish as well.

You see, we weren't really competing against all the other painters. Our niche set us apart. We charged a lot more for our TT&P than mere painters. And our narrow focus developed our skills so "painters" couldn't deliver the quality results we did.

Narrow Your Niche

Until You Stand Out

You can compete with the Big Guys. You may find after all your calculations that you still have to charge more for your TT&P than they do. If this is the case, look for a niche similar to what they offer yet different enough that you stand out. In a narrow niche you can charge more because what you offer is seen as better and more specialized than the Big Guys.

The Grimy Underbelly

You'll have to consider other competitors too. I call them the "Underbelly Competition." These guys won't be so easy to find. The Underbelly are the ones who sell for cheap. They might be selling so cheap it makes your head spin. Every industry has them, even "online" businesses. These guys will do the "same work" you do for half the price. Well, at least they claim to do the same work as you do.

The reason they're harder to find is that the expression "fly-by-night" was created just for these guys. I say they "claim" to do the same work as you do. They don't actually do the same work. They work cheap because they give cheap results.

The Underbelly won't impact how much you have to charge for your TT&P as the Big Guys do. Most of your customers will know cheap prices lead to bad results.

But the Underbelly will derail you psychologically if you let them. You see, you will lose a few sales to the Underbelly. Some people only consider the cheapest price when they buy. You will feel like you've got to drop your price to meet or beat them.

Don't do it! Slap yourself if you start down that road. You just finished putting together a plan. You know your overhead and how much you have to charge. Do you really think you can cut your price? It's insanity to think you can compete with a fly-by-night Underbelly competitor by cutting your price.

Cheap, Cheap, Cheaper

Here's how to deal with these Underbelly competitors. Don't compete on price. Yes, that's what I said. Don't compete on price. You can't win competing on price. Someone will always be willing to sell for less.

The people who sell for cheap are in three categories. The first group includes businesses cutting corners and doing crappy work. Usually they have no insurance, ask to be paid in cash . . . and you may or may not get what they promise to deliver. And did I mention they do crappy work? There's no warranty and no customer service.

The Dumb and Dumber

The second Underbelly group includes businesses on their way to being broke and out of business. These guys didn't do the break-even and profit calculations you just did. They don't have a clue what their overhead is. They may do good work or sell good products, but they won't be around for long because they're not charging enough for their TT&P.

Shoe Money Entrepreneurs

The third group of Underbelly competitors includes business owners who have a spouse or partner supporting them and they just want "shoe money." They may or may not do good work. They may or may not be insured. They're really not interested in building their business. Being self-employed just gives them more freedom and flexibility than working as an employee, and so they treat their business like a hobby.

It's this third category of Underbelly competition that can give you fits. They can offer decent value and quality and still sell the same TT&P you have for cheap. Mind you, they don't all have the kind of professional approach you're going to bring to your business. It's still just a hobby for them. But a few of these "hobby entrepreneurs" may be serious competition.

You're Not Wal-Mart

I'm going to say it again because you've got to hear this: Don't compete on price. This applies to the Big Guys as well as the Underbelly. Don't compete on price.

Some people think buying cheap is the same thing as being frugal. They always buy the cheapest, whether it's a product or a service. It doesn't matter if it's a crappy product or shoddy workmanship; the price is the most important thing to them.

Trust me, you don't want to cater to bargain-basement customers. You need to market to the people who buy value not price. Value shoppers will pay more for good quality. Value shoppers may shop at discount stores for milk and bread, but they'll buy their clothes at Nordstrom, not Wal-mart.

So look at your competition. You know what you've got to charge for your TT&P. Now make a plan for where to carve out your niche so you can be profitable. You have to stand out if you're going to be successful. Your niche market must see you as a better choice than your competitors. Offer a unique value to your market. Do this and you can compete effectively with the Big Guys as well as the Underbelly.

Standing out and showing your value leads us to the next part of business planning: marketing.

Chapter 5

Basic Marketing

You judge a book by the cover, don't you? Yes, I know *they* say not to. But you know everyone does. It's a fact: books with ugly covers don't sell. Of course, you buy more than the cover. The book has to be good too. But you do judge a book by the cover, and everyone else out there does too.

Marketing is the book cover for your business. Marketing is about making you and your business look good to your customers. Just like writing a good book, you've got to deliver what you promise in your marketing. But if you don't look good, no one's going to pay attention to you.

A scene from one of the Mega Mind movies illustrates this point perfectly. As Mega Mind makes his entrance, Metro Man says, "This town isn't big enough for two super villains."

"Oh, you're a villain all right, just not a super one," Mega Mind replies.

"Oh, yeah?" Metro Man says. "What's the difference?"

A huge projection of Mega Mind's face appears out of the clouds and Mega Mind steps forward and declares, "Presentation!"

You can't get the full effect from words alone. Take a minute to look it up and watch it. Search online for the keywords "Mega Mind presentation" and you should find several YouTube clips of this scene.

Who Hears the Tree Fall?

Do you know this question: "If a tree falls in the forest and no one is there to hear it, does it still make a sound?" But here's a more important question: "If a person hears the tree fall but ignores it, does it matter whether the tree makes a sound or not?"

You may be thinking, "What does a tree falling in the woods have to do with marketing?" Just hang in here with me, I'm circling in on my point. Your marketing won't get far if no one pays attention. You've got to be noticed. Getting noticed comes from a good presentation.

Put Yourself Out There

It doesn't matter how good you are. You might be the best in the world. Your TT&P could be so good that your customers would be foolish not to do business with you. None of this means jack unless people know about you.

Your potential customers have to both know about you and believe you're as good as you say. Your customers' opinion of you determines whether or not they will buy anything from you. And what they think of you begins with your marketing.

The Path to Your Door

Have you heard the old saying about the better mousetrap? If you design a better mousetrap people will beat a path to your door to buy it. Don't believe it! No one cares about your door or the path leading to it. They want a mousetrap that works and is easy to buy. Unless your mousetrap is so irresistible that mice flock to it and never return, people are going to just keep using the spring on a board like they always have. Your TT&P must be outstanding — and at the same time, you've got to give an outstanding presentation.

Your New Best Friends

Looking good to your potential customers is not what is commonly called "getting your name out there." I made this mistake. Yes, you're going to have lots of advertising people come to you with this mantra: "You've got to get your name out there."

Let me warn you, the first people who will notice your new business are the advertising sellers. They're going to treat you like they're your new best friends. They may even claim to be "consultants." They'll give you the line about how hordes of your potential customers will see your ad. (That's getting your name out there.)

Let me save you some grief. Salespeople make money selling you ads. They aren't consultants. Don't blindly trust the advice of anyone who is going to profit when you take his or her advice.

The Proverb says there is safety in a multitude of counselors. Get your marketing and advertising advice from experts, not sales people. Don't be afraid to ask the hard questions. The salesperson wants to make a buck and the expert wants to come alongside you to serve you. Know the difference.

I Wanna Talk About Me!

Yes, I'm repeating myself. I want you to get this. Just "getting your name out there" won't do squat for you. Most people don't care who you are. People don't care that you're starting a business you love and have dreamed about for years. People don't care about you at all.

People think about themselves and what they want and how to make their own life comfortable. Yes, people are selfish. And even those who care won't remember your name, the name you're working hard to get out there. It's so much more than that.

Your prospects want to know "What's in it for me?" Your presentation has to be good. And it has to be about them.

You Still Need the Basics

Yes, you'll need to create a logo and brand yourself. Get business cards and color-coordinated marketing materials. Set up a solid website with great content. Make yourself and your business look good to your prospective customers. These might be considered "name-getting-out-there" activities.

But make these decisions quickly and get to the real work of marketing: telling your customers what you can do for them. Your marketing has to hit your customers' hot buttons. Talk to them about what they want.

These Are the Droids You're Looking For

You've got to make your presentation so they'll believe you're the one to give them what they want. Your marketing needs to be like the Jedi mind masters. Present your customers with what they want, not what they need. So begin by thinking about what your customers want and why they buy the things they want.

Don't forget, you're not selling to everyone. You identified your niche back in your business plan. You did that, didn't you? Go back and look at your stack of napkins and find the one about your customers.

Find the one that details who your ideal customer is. (You wrote these details down, didn't you?) You're going to need more than napkins here. Get a pad of paper. Get inside the mind of your ideal customer. Take all those characteristics you know about him or her and find their wants. Most of all, you should know what your ideal customer wants from your business. Why will they buy your TT&P? Find out what's their real motivation to buy from you?

Another Faux Example

I defined our ideal customer and her motivation in my marketing planning. The housing market was hot in the early 2000s. And the demand for faux finishes exploded.

New faux finishers popped up to meet the demand. Most of them marketed their skills to home builders. It seemed like a logical choice. New homeowners want the latest interior design trend.

We taught classes and sold faux finish products back then. Our students went after the new-construction business. We went after a different niche. We marketed to homeowners who had been in their house for at least a few years and were ready to make changes in the decor.

So our ideal client was a woman living in a 3,000 square foot, two-story home in the southwest part of our metro area. She was college educated, but her husband was the primary wage earner. She had two children, usually between 6 and 12 years old. She may work part time, but she also volunteered and was active in clubs and social organizations.

She wanted faux finishes on her walls because the hand-done effect was highly customized to her colors and decorating style. Each project we did was art on the wall, a unique blend of colors with our unique style.

Her friends either already had faux finishes on their walls, or they wanted them. So peer pressure was her motivation to buy our TT&P. She wanted her home to be unique, just like all of her friends' homes. Yes, I know it's a paradox.

None of our clients needed what we sold. But they wanted faux finished walls. And we knew they wanted the status and prestige of showing off their home to their friends.

Back then, the tag line on our business cards said, "We make you look good in your home." We directed our marketing to their reason for buying: social status.

Try and Test

You need this same kind of knowledge about your customers. You'll have to narrow down your niche to find the people who want your TT&P and are willing to pay you what you need to make a profit. You need to know what they want and why they choose to buy.

So once you've got your niche narrowed down and targeted, it's time to look at the nuts and bolts so you can make a plan to tell these eager customers your story.

Test, test, then test some more. Only keep what works.

Your primary objective as an entrepreneur in a small business is to make every bit of your marketing effective. Keep this question in mind as you plan your marketing: What is my return on investment going to be?

Remember our discussion on overhead? You've got to bring in much more in sales than you spend on advertising to just break even. Yes, your marketing and advertising is part of your overhead. But you're losing money if you only bring in $1,000 in sales after you spend $1,000 in advertising.

Marketing and Multiplication

Go back and look at the number you have for your overhead. Your marketing budget is part of this number. Let's say your marketing budget is 10% of your total overhead. Are you with me so far?

So, you're going to spend that 10% to generate enough sales to bring in the other 90% in addition to getting back the 10% you spend.

Keep in mind: your overhead and budgets are annual. Don't expect your advertising and marketing to produce an immediate exponential return. You couldn't handle that much business all at once anyway.

I do want you to see that your advertising and marketing has to be highly effective. Your results need to return your investment and multiplied returns. You're wasting time and money if your advertising isn't getting exponential results.

Track Your Marketing

Here's the pickle about advertising: you have to try it before you know whether or not it works. Salespeople will tell you, "This ad campaign is great! You'll get tons of calls."

They'll promise you the moon and the stars and the kitchen sink. They may be able to deliver what they promise. But, then again, they may be selling you a pig in a poke. Believe me, it's no fun to spend a boatload of money on advertising and get absolutely nothing. Yep, been there. Done that.

Do As I Say, Not As I Did

One year, I spent thousands of dollars on advertising in a home magazine and got zip-zero-nada. It wasn't just that I got no business from the ads. I did get one call, from someone asking advice on what color to paint her kitchen. Not our target market. But I did get lots of calls from other advertising salespeople who saw my ad and wanted me to spend money to advertise in their magazine.

My next advertising failure came when I bought leads from an online company. They promised to send pre-qualified leads from people wanting home-improvement services.

I'll spare you the gory details. Suffice it to say, it was a disaster (or insert your favorite profanity). In fact, it was so bad for me that I'll tell you categorically that if someone tries to sell you some kind of online lead referral service, just say no.

And furthermore, my standard answer is NO to anyone who calls trying to sell me advertising that's not part of my marketing strategy already.

Now, of course, my response is colored by my experience. I know what doesn't work for me. And I spent a lot of time and money learning what doesn't work.

In hindsight, I should have chosen smaller ad campaigns and tested my results first, before I spent the big money. I still get calls from salespeople selling advertising I've proven to be ineffective for me. Salespeople can be pushy. But I'm a rock. I won't budge, because I know better now.

Find What Doesn't Work

Remember how I said that learning to fail quickly and fail well is part of your job as an entrepreneur?

Marketing is one area in which you'll fail your way to success. You won't know what works and what doesn't when you start. Don't fail big, like I did. Fail small. Whatever marketing strategy you use, test it always. If it doesn't work or gives you crappy results, scrap it and try something else.

Yes, Make a Marketing Plan

You should write a rough draft of your marketing plan when you do your budget. Yes, I know you already listed the money in your budget, right? Your marketing plan is where you figure out how to spend that money to get those exponential returns I talked about. So go back and look at your budget and put together an initial marketing plan based on that number.

Know that your marketing budget is just an estimate. And, by the way, you'll have to adjust a lot of your budget once it meets the harsh reality of the real world. Once you get your business running you'll make adjustments. Don't sweat it for now. But I digress.

Keep it Simple

I think it's a good rule of thumb to make your initial marketing plan both simple and as frugal as possible. Marketing can become a black hole that sucks up your money, energy and time. This is especially true if your only experience with marketing is as a customer.

You'll be tempted to compare your marketing efforts with all the advertising you see from established businesses. You've got to remember: their budget is a lot bigger than your budget. I'll talk about marketing tactics in a bit. But first, let's look at some basic marketing decisions you'll need to make.

What's In a Name?

Picking a business name is like naming a child. You've heard of parents who gave their children odd names. Dweezil and Moon Unit Zappa come to mind. Frank Zappa is famous (at least he was). I guess he can justify naming his kids odd names. Search Google for a list of the oddest baby names. Here are a few from the 2012 list: Espn, Htoo, Ummi and Rilo. I chose two boy names and two girl names, in case you wondered.

You may never admit it, but you judge people you meet by their name. You may have read studies of how the name on a resume determines the odds of whether a person is considered for a job.

People make the same kinds of judgments about business names too. You need to consider all of this when you choose your business name.

So think long and hard about what to call your business. Don't just draw names out of a hat. Remember, your customer's first impression is your business name.

It's also the first hurdle to get your customer's attention. And your business name should give prospective customers an idea of what your business is about.

Pick a name people can grab hold of and remember. You don't want your prospects dithering in their minds wondering if you've got what they want. A confused mind always says "no."

The "Do I Need You?" Question

Take, for example, the business named "Seasonal Concepts." What do you suppose they do? Does their name let you know whether you need their services? They are a local company, and I've heard their ads on the radio. But, at the moment, I don't recall what they do.

You want to be like the guys at "Guier Fence." I've heard their ads too. I know to call them if I need a fence. Maybe Seasonal Concepts offers fencing, as well as whatever else is "seasonal." But who will I remember when the neighbor's dog poops in my yard one too many times? I'll be calling Guier Fence to get over here right now so I can keep that mutt off my property.

You may lean toward a unique name with "creative flair." Be careful. It's okay to be creative, but make sure it passes the eight-year-old test. Tell it to a child eight years old or younger. If the child gets it, you've got a winner. "Robert's Currency Preservation and Management

Company" may sound high class, but "Bob's Bank" leaves no room for doubt.

Don't Do as I Did

The original title of this book was *Stop Your Paycheck Addiction.* I had positive feedback from friends, family and my online master-mind group. It sounded like a winner. But my wife wasn't thrilled with it. I ignored her and went along with the majority who agreed with me.

It turns out my wife was right . . . again. In the crush of Amazon titles, mine wasn't clear. A confused mind says "no".

Choose a Logo

The next step in your basic marketing is to get a logo. A logo is part of your "branding." Branding is the process of creating an image and an identity for your business.

You are the brand when you start your business. Your customers will "buy" you. Your business may grow to establish its own brand identity, apart from you. But some business brands remain tied to an individual or group. Consider the brand Kim Kardashian created. Or look at the Duck Dynasty TV show. These brands are tightly linked to individuals, for better or worse.

So your logo is important because it's one part of creating your brand as a business. You can easily get tied up in knots trying to get it just right. But if you obsess over getting it perfect, you're spending energy and time you need elsewhere. Don't just throw out some generic, half-baked logo. But keep it simple and get it done. You can change your logo later if you want to. My business has had several over the years.

Here are some ideas to keep in mind to help you choose a logo. Use graphics to enhance or complement your business name. Sometimes, you can use your business name with creative fonts for a dynamite logo. Just be sure to make it easy for your customers to understand. Your logo should enhance your name, not detract from it.

Now I'm a do-it-yourself type. I do things myself to be frugal. But don't try to do create a logo on your own unless you're a graphic designer. Hire someone. Research prices to find out what a good quality graphic designer charges. Shop around and hire the best you can afford.

For the most cost-effective solution, check for freelance design resources online. You can find graphic designers from around the world to bid on your logo project. Another option is to check with a local community college and see if someone in their graphic design program wants to do a real life project for his or her portfolio.

Just be sure your logo design and the font of the text is easily readable. Don't use script fonts. Script fonts are hard to read. People need to be able to quickly read and understand your name and logo. You've got less than two seconds to get their attention.

Also, keep in mind that you'll likely want to put your name and logo on a sign, poster or vehicle. Make sure it's easy to read from a distance. Believe me, people will only ignore your sign if it's not easy to read.

Your Customers Expect a Website

It used to be that no one took you seriously in business if you didn't have a business address. "Real" businesses had a "brick and mortar" address. Your home-based business was not much more than a hobby — at least, that was the prevailing attitude. That attitude is ancient history now.

The thing that defines a "real" business today is your web address. I've met some entrepreneurs who still don't have a website. But, in most cases, your customers are going to expect you to have something about your business on the Internet.

Now, you may be one of the thousands of entrepreneurs who start a web-based business. Your TT&P may be "virtual" so that you can market and operate your business from your desktop.

You've probably gathered that my focus is on "offline" small businesses and, more specifically, a business providing a service to customers. But what I'm showing you can be used for any kind of business. Because simple, easy-to-start small businesses use the basic fundamentals needed in every business, I'm focusing on "non-tech" businesses. Of course, you can translate these business principles to apply to an online business too.

Online and tech-related businesses are good if you have the right skills. But you may be like me and enjoy creating stuff and working with your hands. Or, you may not want to be tied to a computer keyboard all day. You can turn all kinds of non-tech skills into a profitable business. But even if you've got the most non-technical business imaginable, your customers will expect a website.

Website Basics

You can find libraries of books about marketing your business online. So I'm not going to put everything you need to know in this section. I will, however, give you a guideline you should use to keep from getting lost in the weeds.

1. Get your own domain name.

2. Keep your design simple.

3. Beware of "SEO experts."

4. Keep it simple.

5. Hire it done.

6. Keep it simple.

Beware of SEO Experts

For years, Internet marketers have played a cat-and-mouse game called search engine optimization (SEO). The "experts" of SEO will claim they can get your website to show up on the first page when someone searches for your business. I believe there are only a handful who can actually deliver on their promises. Many so-called experts use shortcuts and questionable tactics. Search engine companies then close the loopholes and the SEO experts work to find new ones. Google recently overhauled their search engine, and some of the old SEO tactics can now actually hurt your website search rank. So beware of SEO experts.

Yes, Hire Someone

Remember all the stuff I told you a minute ago about creating a logo yourself? All of that applies to your website too. You may be able to cobble together a website. And there are plenty of free tools out there. You can stitch together some text and graphics and throw it on the web.

But just like logos are best left to graphic designers, your website needs a web developer. And the same stuff I said about finding someone to design a logo applies to your website. You don't have to spend a fortune. Use a little creative thinking and find the best web designer you can afford.

The Most Important Part of Your Business

Your money and your marketing are the two vital parts of your business. I repeat this phrase so you'll remember it's important. You need to manage both well if you hope to be a successful entrepreneur.

Remember, be careful how you spend your money and deploy your marketing. You're in business to get a return on your investment. Your money can take wings and fly away if you don't track your expenses and the effectiveness of your marketing.

Chapter 6

Relationship Marketing

If you have a large marketing budget, that's great! You have lots of options if you've got plenty of money. But the rest of us need every dollar we can scrape together. And those dollars have to stretch as far as possible.

In general, the more money you put into your marketing the better off you'll be. That is, you'll be better off if you put your money into effective marketing. As I've already mentioned, at the minimum, your marketing plan needs to include business cards and a website.

Who Do You Know?

One of the best marketing tactics you can use is to network with everyone you know and ask for referrals. Supposedly, only six degrees of separation stand between you and any other random person on the planet. So you know people who know people who need your product or service.

Referrals are your least expensive way to market your business. Referrals are also the most effective marketing you can do. You'll hear a lot of small business owners say they rely on "word of mouth" to bring them business. "Word of mouth" is another word for referrals. But unless you have a plan to make it work, word of mouth isn't reliable or consistent.

You can buy complex training programs and systems that teach you how to build your business by referral. But when you're starting your business, you need just a bare-bones plan you can get up and running quickly.

Use a System

The most important aspect of using referrals (word of mouth) to market your business is to track where your new customers come from. Remember, the two things you've got to pay attention to in business are your marketing and your money.

You've got to know what works and what doesn't in your marketing. So ask every prospect and customer how he or she found out about you. Write their answers down. You can make notes in a spiral notebook, or use a variety of computer tools for keeping this info. Find a tracking system you like and try it out. If it doesn't work for you, find another you like better.

The main thing is to have a plan to keep track of where you're getting new customers — and you especially want to keep track of the people you get from referrals.

The second thing you'll need to track are the people who send you referrals. You don't want to rely on accidental referrals from some nameless source. You need to know who's referring you because you're going to say "thank you" to them. It's a great honor when someone trusts you enough to send a friend or relative to buy your TT&P. Send a thank you card or give these folks a call.

Ask And You Will Receive

So how do you get a list of people who'll talk about you and send you business? It's simple: you ask them to refer you.

Now, you may feel a bit nervous about asking people to refer you. You don't want to come across like some cheesy used car salesman. So you should start with your good friends and family. I would hope that they already like you and want to see you succeed.

Next, talk to acquaintances. These are people who will probably recognize you in the grocery store and wave, but they don't really know you all that well. These are the ones who are harder to ask. Sure, they're all smiles when you wave at them, but you never know if they really like you or not.

So here's a way to ask those kinds of people for referrals. And this line will even work just as well for someone you've met for the first time, like at a networking event or party.

Can I Be Your Guy / Gal?

You usually talk about your job somewhere in the course of a conversation. Whether you've just met someone or you're catching up with a friend, work is a prime topic. You need to develop an "elevator pitch." An elevator pitch is a 30-second explanation of what your business is all about. Imagine explaining your TT&P to someone in the time it takes for an elevator to go between floors. Think of it as a verbal text message – compact and filled with vital information.

In a conversation, you can also tell this person a little about your reason for starting your business and the unique service or product you offer. Then let them respond and, hopefully, ask questions. If they say, "Oh, that's nice," and change the subject or walk away, they probably aren't a good prospect for referrals.

But if they respond and talk a little about your new business, ask them this question: **"If one of your friends needs ___ (the service or product you provide), do you know someone you can refer them to?"** This is a yes or no question. If the person says "no," you then ask if you can keep in touch with them and be their source for your product or service. Usually they will say, "yes."

Promise them, and promise me, that you won't spam them. Tell them you want to keep them informed about your business and give them information so they can better explain your product or service to their friends.

Have a Backup Plan

On the other hand, this person you're talking to may already "have a guy / gal." These people answer "yes" when you ask them if they know someone they refer. But they usually don't just say "yes" . . . most of the time they give the name of another business (possibly one of your competitors). And they'll tell you valuable information about your competitor, so listen closely to what they say.

Ask questions and get as much information about these competitors as you can. If this business they mention does exactly the same thing you do, then file the information in your mind and say "thank you." Don't blow it off. The information you just got is priceless.

But you might find this person is talking about a business that doesn't do exactly what you do. Or they may do some of the things you do, but you've got a specialty niche product or service they don't provide. Or they may not serve the same area of town you serve.

Hear me on this, never try to convince someone to refer you instead of someone they already have a history with. Here is your best strategy. Look for gaps you can fill in. Ask this person to refer you in the places you don't compete with the guys they already refer.

For example, imagine you're starting a cleaning business. And let's suppose your target niche includes families with homes 2,500 square feet or less. And let's suppose you ask an acquaintance if they know a house cleaning business they refer and they say "yes." They have a relationship with someone who'll be your competitor.

But suppose by asking for details about your competition you find that the business your acquaintance refers only serves the north side of your city and prefers large homes: 3,000 square feet and bigger.

If your target market is the south side and you're going after smaller homes, you can still ask this person for referrals. You're not asking them to quit referring your competition. You're only asking them to remember you for the niche you serve and the other business doesn't.

No Selling Allowed

Now hear me on this: don't try to convince people you know to be your customers. Making a sales pitch to everyone you know will make you a social leper. Ask for referrals instead.

This will do two things. The people you talk to won't be in the awkward position to tell you "no" when they don't want what you're selling. Rather than being offended, they'll be flattered that you consider them a person of influence. And the funny thing is that they'll buy from you if they want your TT&P.

I'm sure there's a psychological explanation for this phenomenon. People who will flat refuse to listen to your sales pitch will turn around and buy from you if you talk about their friends who might want your stuff.

Just put yourself in the other person's shoes. Think how you feel when someone tries to sell you something. Do feel the resistance building up in your gut even now? The same thing happens to your friends when you accost them with a sales pitch.

But imagine someone asking you for an introduction to your circle of influence. They tell you about their TT&P. They ask if you know anyone interested. It's easy for you think about buying from them because you "discovered" something you want in a non-threatening context.

Now, I'm not suggesting you use this tactic as a ploy to sell to the people you know. Be honest and serious in your request for referrals. If the people you know want to buy from you, then that's just a bonus.

You probably know about 150 or so people. A handful of them will be potential customers. But each of the people you know also knows 150 — that's 22,500 prospects. That's a boat-load of potential customers, enough to keep you busy for a while.

Sort Your List

Okay, so you've learned how to ask for referrals. And you've set up your systems to track who's referring you. Your next step is to keep an organized list of the people most likely to refer you.

People will be nice to you. They'll usually agree to refer you when you ask them nicely. And most of them really do intend to refer you. But they quickly forget about you.

On the other hand, some of them will be lying to you. The liars aren't being mean. In fact, they're trying to be polite.

They're too afraid to tell you to your face that they really don't like any of their friends and no one ever listens to their recommendations anyway. They may not really like you all that much either. Or they may have a flock of reasons they agree to refer you but don't.

So you're going to need a list to separate the people who won't refer you from the ones who might refer you and the ones who really will refer you.

And here's how to categorize them. Divide your list into four categories: A, B, C, D.

A-list people are your Advocates, the people who have already referred you or you know will refer you. Your mom should be first on this list, at least I hope your mom likes you.

B-list people are your Buddies. These are people who are likely to refer you. C-list people are the Crowd. These are people who might refer you, but you're not sure if they will or not. D stands for "Deadbeat" and "Delete."

Some people won't refer you, ever. They say "yes" because they don't want to look like a loser and tell you "no." Don't go and lose any sleep over your D-list. Just let them fade quietly away and concentrate on the good people who like you and are willing to talk about you.

New people on your list start as Bs or Cs, depending on your gut feeling about how likely they are to actually refer you.

As you develop your list, your goal is to move people from the Crowd to Advocates. Some people will surprise you. You'll get referrals from some you didn't expect, and you'll end up Deleting some people you thought were sure to be Advocates. Remember, ask all your prospects and customers how they found you. Use that information to move people on your referral list into the appropriate category.

Your Best People

Make a special category for the people who refer you a lot. You can call this your AA list. These are your Awesome Advocates. Take good care of these people. Let them know how much you appreciate them. Keep in touch with them, and find extra creative ways to say thank you . . . and not just when they refer you.

Remember birthdays and holidays, and recognize them with a card or gift. Make a plan for keeping in touch with them and never miss a chance to let them know how much they mean to you.

Now, don't go overboard, calling them every week. But you've got to make the effort to get to know them, what they like, their hobbies and interests. Send them a note or give them a call if you run across information or news you know hits their sweet spot.

Be Top of Mind

So how do you stay in touch with these people after you've promised them you will? You should have a good idea how your ideal customers communicate. Depending on your niche, you could use any one of a combination of the following: paper newsletter in the mail, email newsletter, short emails with links, personal phone calls, personal visits or texts.

If you do business with your customers face-to-face, a paper newsletter may get more attention than an email. If most of your business is online, it might make sense to do an email newsletter. If you're sending a paper newsletter in the mail, you can do it as often as once a month. But, in my opinion, sending it out quarterly strikes a good balance between staying in touch and being an over-attached, needy person no one wants to hear from anymore.

I Wanna Talk About Me

You can find whole books written about this kind of marketing, and experts equipped to guide you through it, so I'm just giving you the "broad brush" treatment here. But here is one thing you need to keep in mind: You've got to make your newsletter (or email) interesting for your customers. Don't make it all about you!

Realtors are notorious for sending out advertising that's "me, me, ME." Remember, people don't care about you. People don't care about your business. They care about themselves. They're like the guy on a first date who spends an hour talking about himself and then says, "I shouldn't be talking about myself so much. What do you like about me?"

Any smart woman will dump this guy and run. You don't want to be this guy.

But your customers are a lot like this guy. You need to play along if you want your customers to love you. Talk about them. Put their wants and desires in your conversation. The art of marketing is to weave yourself and your business into the conversation about them.

Are You Valuable?

Give information related to your industry: news and trends. Include a little bit about how you're keeping on top of the changes and working to provide cutting edge service and products. But make sure you give customers a benefit they can use.

For example, some Realtors sent me newsletters showing average selling prices of houses in my neighborhood as well as how many houses sold. Keep in mind, these weren't necessarily houses they had sold. It was sales data they compiled from their sources. I always read these because I was interested in how valuable my own home was, even though I wasn't ready to sell my home right then.

Make your marketing and advertising like these successful Realtors' newsletters. Whatever you send to your referral list needs to be something they'll value and want to see.

Before the advent of the "forever" stamps, I sent a notice to my referral list whenever the post office raised their rates. I included a book of one or two-cent stamps -- whatever the rate increase was. Those letters got more response than any other letter I sent.

One man called me and said, "You saved my butt. I had a letter that had to go out today and I didn't have any of the new stamps." I love getting those kinds of calls, and I was sad when the post office came out with "forever" stamps. For your customers and your referral list, make it a priority to give them outstanding value in everything you do.

You also need to remember the people on your list won't have the same passion for your industry as you do.

Be happy if they have a mild interest, enough to read your newsletter. The main thing is you want them to see you as the expert. You want them to think of you whenever your product or service is mentioned.

People will refer you if you just ask. But you'll be better off if you coach them on how to refer you.

They can refer you in one of three ways. No one way is better than the others. But you should think about what way would work best for you then test it out.

Give Me a Lead

The first way you can get referrals is ask the people on your list to send you leads. This means they call you with their friend's name so you can then call their friend.

The benefit here is this method gives you a point of contact with the people on your referral list. You know exactly who's referring you the most. It makes it easy to classify the people on your list into the A, B, C, and D categories.

The weakness of this method is that leads often put you in the role of a salesperson when you call. Yes, it gives you more control. You're not just waiting for the other person to call. But the interaction feels different when you call.

Now, the person who referred you should have already talked you up to his or her friend. But you never know how motivated this referral is when you make that initial call. Depending on your personality and your industry, this method of receiving referrals might work well for you.

Here's My Number, Call Me Maybe

The second way to receive referrals is less structured. Ask the people in your referral list to pass your name on to people who want your TT&P.

The advantage of prospects calling you is that the interaction feels less like a sales call. These calls aren't just leads: these people have taken action. They picked up the phone and called you.

The disadvantage to this method is you have to be diligent to link prospects back to the person on your referral list who sent them to you. And you have to remember to reach out to thank that person for remembering you.

This second method of receiving referrals is also more passive. You're relying on people on your list to spur their friends into action. Their friends may get your name and still not call you; they may find someone else to do business with. They may change their mind. You won't get the chance to call the referral and sell yourself. You probably won't even know a referral happened if the friend never calls.

But this method is better if you're not a strong salesperson, or if your Advocates are stronger salespeople than you are. Those who call have raised their hand and said, "I'm interested in what you've got to offer." So your sales process isn't so much convincing them to buy your TT&P. You're more of an adviser, helping them decide how your TT&P can help them best.

Introduce Me Please

The third method to receive referrals is to ask for introductions. The people who refer you are the middlemen and contact both you and the person they're referring.

Ask them to contact you by phone or email and give you information about the person they're introducing you to. Ask them to also give your information to the person they're referring and let them know they should talk to you.

This kind of introduction sets up an expectation between you and the person being referred that you're going to be in contact. It also frames the initial contact as that of a meeting rather than a sales call. This introduction sets you up as an adviser, helping the person who's being referred to get what they want.

This third method has all the advantages of the first two, with none of the disadvantages. I like being introduced. It's better than just a passive referral.

People Will Talk

You can use this relationship marketing method with almost any business you start. Yes, people will refer you if you do good work. But the way to make word of mouth marketing work for you is to be intentional about your referral system. And that means you have to ask for referrals.

Don't be pushy, but don't be shy about it either. Your best sources for referrals are the people you're doing business with right now. You're at the top of their mind. They see the value of your TT&P and see how well you deliver on your promises. You also need to consider the excellence and skill you put into your TT&P as part of your marketing.

Your goal should be to give such outstanding service that your customers will remember you for years. But the customers you're serving right now are the ones thinking about you the most. Train yourself to talk about referrals in your sales process, and remember to ask for referrals when you've completed the job or delivered the goods to your customer.

Universally Adaptable

Relationship marketing works whether you do business face-to-face or online. The key is interacting with your customers. Give them an outstanding experience when they do business with you.

Most people think of business by referral only for service-related businesses: finding a contractor, hiring someone to clean your home, etc. But you can tweak this system to work in any business. Just take the concepts and apply some creative thinking and make this method your own.

Generating referrals is one of the best and cost-effective kinds of marketing you can use. But it's smart to try other marketing strategies as well.

Chapter 7

Guerrilla Marketing

Guerrilla fighters use low-budget weapons and unconventional tactics to fight against larger forces. When effective, their strategy brings political change. Their goal along the way is to also win the hearts and minds of the people.

Guerrilla marketing, like guerrilla warfare, uses low budget tools and methods. The strategy is the same. You expect small and inexpensive efforts to produce big results. Your strategy also is to win the hearts and minds of your niche market.

Guerrilla marketing reaches your niche market with as little wasted effort and expense as possible. In short, it's finding where your ideal customers are then targeting them with the most inexpensive and effective methods.

I've listed several guerrilla marketing tactics in this chapter. Some of these I've used. Some I just know about. The relationship marketing I describe in the previous chapter is one of the most effective marketing methods in my business. But I know other entrepreneurs who've had great success with the guerrilla marketing methods described here.

Flyers and Door Hangers

Putting flyers on doors is one of the oldest guerrilla marketing techniques. It was effective back when there were only rotary dial phones. And you can trace this strategy back several centuries. Martin Luther posted his ideas on the church door in the year 1517 and began the Protestant movement.

It still works today. It's an inexpensive way to reach your niche market. Devote a few hours a week to distributing your flyers and you might get a good return on your investment. Here are a couple of tips for using flyers.

First, be consistent. This is true for any marketing you do. Make a plan and keep doing it. Remember to test your plan: start small. If it doesn't work, try something else. It's better to use flyers a little at a time consistently than a huge blitz every once in a while. Start with a few hours each week for however many weeks you want to run your test. If this works, keep doing it a couple of hours each week.

Second, and it should be obvious, but I need to say it anyway. You need to have a good flyer. You can buy books about designing good flyers. These will be good investments if you decide to use flyers. These books will give you valuable pointers, like where on the page is the most effective place to put your logo, and how to write compelling advertising copy. Your flyer needs to look good, but even a black and white photocopy can get results if you pay attention to design and good copy.

Here are four qualities your flyer should have, at the very least:

1. *It has to be easy to read.* Too much text and overload of graphics and your message goes straight in the trash. You're lucky if your flyer gets a quick glance en route to the recycling bin. Make your message pop. Make it memorable in five seconds or less.

2. *Introduce yourself, but talk about them.* In fact, talk about them even before you introduce yourself. Make the headline a hook to get their attention and show them a benefit. Then talk about what you do. Tell how your TT&P will benefit them.

For example, if your business is home organizing, you might say: *"How much time and money can you save when your home is professionally organized?"* This headline asks a question . . . and curiosity is a powerful psychological hook. The main thing is that it's about them.

3. *Start a conversation, but don't try to sell.* No one decides to buy because of your flyer. You want the reader to think enough of your offer to contact you -- or at least consider your offer. Your flyer scores when someone is intrigued enough to look you up online, send an email, call, etc. You sell after you have their attention. Even then, your sales process should feel more like a conversation than a sales pitch.

4. *Make an offer.* Give them a reason to contact you. An offer isn't just a special discount or coupon. Coupons can work, but your offer could be information or free advice. An offer is a call to action: a compelling reason for them to contact you. Staying with the example of a home organization business, your offer could be a free, no-obligation analysis of the time and money they can save by being professionally organized.

Your offer is the most important part of your flyer. Most of us are lazy. We won't put out the effort to buy something until it's a near emergency. A good offer gets your prospect over this hurdle. Make it worthwhile for them to call.

Clear it With City Hall

Be sure to check your local ordinances before you begin. Some cities may require a permit before you can distribute flyers. And in some areas, it's not allowed at all. I've heard of entrepreneurs hit with hefty fines because they didn't know the rules, so do your research.

Bandit Signs

You've seen these signs stuck along the side of the road or nailed to power poles. They advertise everything from "We Buy Houses" to cleaning services to house painting to weight-loss plans. They're called "Bandit Signs" for a reason. In most cities, it's against the law to put up signs like these.

Some cities will fine you for bandit signs. And in some cities you can face criminal charges. So I'm not advocating that you break the law. And my lawyer advises I clarify this point: any example I use about bandit signs is hypothetical and doesn't come from personal experience. (*Wink, wink. Nudge, nudge.*)

Bandit signs won't work for every business. But in the city where I live, the local "1-800-Got Junk" franchise built his business using them. I couldn't drive anywhere without seeing one of his signs, usually on an entrance ramp to the interstate. I asked him if he got fined very often. He said, "I'm glad to pay the fines because I get tons of business from those signs." He considered the cost of the fines as his marketing budget.

One strategy I've used — *I mean, one strategy I've heard about* — is to put out bandit signs on a Friday afternoon and pick them up on Sunday night. The sign police are government employees who don't work on weekends. People see your message all weekend, and you have a low risk of getting in trouble.

This strategy shields you from "official" trouble. But you may still lose signs because people don't like seeing them in the neighborhood. These folks will pull your signs and trash them. You might even get some angry calls. But you probably will avoid paying fines if you get your signs pulled up by Sunday night.

Pay attention here. Make sure your sign is on public property if you ever decide to plop one down somewhere. Remember, you're leaving your phone number as well as evidence you were there. It's not good if you're also trespassing on private property.

But if you have a friend or relative living where people from your niche market will drive by, you might ask permission to put a sign in their yard. And if you do service-related work in homes, like painting, cleaning, mindless games or to connect with a few select friends and family.

Twitter claims 200 million active users as of the date this is written. But that doesn't mean any of them will pay attention when you Tweet.

Social media may not be effective for you. Even if it is, you'll work harder and spend more time developing an effective social media strategy than you will other marketing methods.

Have a Plan and Offer Value

The key word here is "strategy." Yes, you need a plan for your marketing, especially online and social media marketing. And it's easy to just jump in and start "doing" social media and think you're marketing. You could be only spinning your wheels.

Social media experts say "engagement" is key. Everyone is tired of "push marketing;" that is, when your message is "Buy my stuff!" Make people feel like you're talking just to them. Don't treat them as if they're part of the herd.

Engagement means interaction. You listen and respond in ways they feel as if their opinion matters. Endlessly promoting yourself and your business on social landscaping, etc., ask your clients if you can put a sign in their yard while you're working on their home.

Remember, you want to reach people in your niche market. If you're working in a neighborhood where your customers live, a sign in the yard is a low-cost way to get the attention of more people in your niche market.

Social Media and Internet

You may wonder why I included social media last? You might think it's a no-brainer to use free tools such as Facebook, Instagram, Snapchat and Twitter. Social media at first appears to be the ultimate guerrilla marketing tool: It's free. You can reach millions.

But remember your strategy. You expect time and money in marketing to give an exponential return in paying customers. Social media will be great if your market niche is all on Facebook, Twitter or some other platform.

Social media is deceptive because it's free. It's a lot of fun. It's also easy to get sidetracked, and before you know it you've spent 45 minutes looking at funny cat videos.

Facebook alone claims over one billion users. People in your niche market may use Facebook, but how do they use it? They may only use Facebook to play media platforms will get you ignored, deleted and "unliked."

You have to remember it's *social* media. Social media is relationship marketing online. The same principles of interaction, connection, offering value and giving appreciation apply here as well.

You have to make it worth their while to be your friend or follow you. Talk about what they care about. Position yourself and your TT&P in the context of their passion. Yes, I know you were paying attention in the previous chapter. I'm repeating myself here. The medium is different. The principle is the same. Talk about them.

Real-World Social Media Examples

I follow a food truck on Twitter. They only have cupcakes. Their Twitter handle is "The Cupcake Cruiser." They tweet out their location and mention how long they'll be there. They update Twitter every time they change locations. They also tweet flavors of the week and flavors they've sold out each day. Sometimes they'll say there are only a few left of a particular flavor.

A local towing company tweets road conditions when bad weather arrives. They also tweet traffic backups or accident locations. This tactic is a bit more generic than the cupcake ladies, but it still offers value for their followers.

What I want you to see from these examples is that social media is about relationships and offering value. Social media isn't a platform to broadcast your message and promote yourself.

Think of it like this: if you're at a party and only talk about yourself all the time, people listen politely for a few seconds and then actively ignore you. Soon, people will turn away when you walk up.

Social media platforms are like huge cocktail parties. Start promoting yourself without connecting with others and engaging in community? You'll be shunned.

Content Marketing

Content marketing is the new catch phrase to describe blogging. (Technically it has a wider meaning than just "blogging." But I think it's close enough a definition for our discussion.) I think content marketing is a good term, and easier to grasp than "blogging."

Think of it as a part of your social media strategy. You produce content showing your experience and expertise concerning your TT&P. You create valuable information for your niche market. You use social media platforms to help your niche find it and converse with you as the "expert."

It's a simple strategy. The tools are inexpensive. But don't confuse *simple* for *easy*. Mike Alton is a social media consultant at www.thesocialmediahat.com. Consider this blog post headline, "How to Find Content Marketing Success in 15 Hours a Week."

Think about it: you could spend 15 hours a week creating content and a couple hours a day on social media. Can you afford 15 – 20 hours a week for "free" marketing? Remember how I said to figure 30 "billable" hours is full time? Spend 50 hours on just marketing and working for money and you won't have time to meet with clients, do your books, etc.

Yes, you can hire freelancers to run content marketing and social media campaigns for you. But make sure you have a strategy and plan in place first. Know the why and how as well as the results you want before you hire help for your marketing.

Remember, no one cares as much about your money or your marketing as you do.

Online Advertising

You can pay for online ads. Paid ads have the advantage of hitting as narrow a niche as you choose. Facebook and Google have tons of data on who their audience is and how to reach them.

Both Facebook and Google constantly change their algorithms (the math formula that decides what you see on their site) to filter your content to the audience they want to serve. You can go crazy trying to create a content marketing strategy that goes to your target niche for free.

The party line from Facebook and Google is they want to give their audience the best user experience possible. But you and I both know it's more about making it so advertisers like us have to pay to reach our audience.

Even so, paid ads could be cheaper for you in the long run. You can set your budget and pick your ideal customer to see your ad.

Marketing Wrap-Up

Invest as much money and time in your marketing plan as you can afford. Test every marketing and advertising tactic you use. Ask: "Will this strategy make people want to buy from me?" And don't forget to test your results. Yes, I'm repeating myself, because this is important.

Again, test your results. Ask everyone how they found out about you. Keep track of the things that work. Keep doing the things that work. Scrap what doesn't work. Tweak your plan and see if your results improve.

Increase your budget as your business grows. Try new strategies as you can afford to. Duplicate and repeat

Chapter 8

Start Up Money

Positive cash flow takes time. You won't just jump into business and be profitable. Well, it's not likely anyway. You'll need cash reserves to keep your business going while you're starting out. Go back and look at the napkin you wrote your business plan on. (Or look at your computer file, if you're the organized one.) Part of your plan needs to include an estimate of how long it will take you to break even and then turn a profit.

The longer it takes to break even, the more cash reserves you'll need. Sounds obvious, right? You probably don't have the luxury of companies like Amazon or Twitter, both of which went for years without turning a profit. And those two companies burned through tons of cash when they were starting up. You'll burn through your start up cash faster than you ever imagined too.

But you may be like I was, with no real cash reserves. So how do you get started when you have no money to start?

Borrowing Start Up Money

You probably already thought of this one. Borrowing money is the "typical" path entrepreneurs take to fund their startup. You can find several government agencies and private foundations dedicated to loaning money for startup businesses. Of course, these people aren't just going to hand you money. They'll want a formal business plan, so collect your napkins with all your notes and put your plans in the format they expect.

Some of these agencies and foundations require you to take business classes and training before they loan you money. By all means, take classes and learn as much as you can. But don't think for a minute you're going to learn everything you need to know. It was an ancient Greek mercenary who said, "It's one thing to study war. It's another to live a warrior's life." Book learning is good, but you'll find real-life business is more complex than what's described in any book.

And as a side note: check the credentials of anyone offering to teach you about business. You won't have this option for lender-required training; you'll have to take whatever you get in that case. But when you have the option, ask if the instructors have ever run a real business.

Find teachers who can teach more than book knowledge. You want to get the nitty-gritty, the here's-my-story information of real-world experience.

I don't have first-hand knowledge about funding a startup with a traditional loan. I did come close when we considered moving our business and ourselves to Iowa. I started the process of making a traditional business plan so I could apply for a small business loan. Our move would have been like a startup, even though I'd been in business five years in my hometown.

Our plans changed and I was glad to toss my vain attempts at a traditional business plan in the trash.

This experience led me to form an opinion about traditional lenders: they only follow traditional guidelines. New ideas and untested markets are a hard sell if you're dealing with traditional business lenders.

Part of our business plan was to offer faux finishing. The faux finish market was a microscopic niche in the mid 1990s. I couldn't find any data to project sales. Faux finish artists operated such small business as to be almost invisible. You had to know someone who knew someone who knew someone in the right circles. Then you might be able to find a referral to a faux finisher.

The traditional lenders wanted hard numbers: market analysis and sales projections. My wife and I just had our gut instinct and limited experience to tell us the demand for faux finishes was building. History proved us right. The faux finish market exploded. But the market was saturated with competitors by the time sales numbers were enough to satisfy traditional lenders.

Based on my limited experience, I offer this advice. Traditional business lenders might be a good fit when you have a business plan that fits in their matrix. Pursue this option if you like. But keep in mind what I said about failing fast. Pull the plug and move on if you find out it's not going to work out. Your other options might be better.

Crowd Funding

Have you ever seen names engraved in bricks making up a sidewalk or patio? People donate money to fund a project and get their name listed on a brick. The bricks and the project they represent are an example of crowd funding.

Crowd funding is nothing new, but the Internet made it available for average folks like you and me. Kickstarter, Indiegogo, and Crowdfunder are a few of the crowd funding sites available at the time this book is being written.

You can use crowd funding for all kinds of projects, including businesses. Each crowd funding site has its own restrictions on the kinds of projects you can create. In general, crowd funding involves uploading your presentation on the crowd funding website. Then, people look at it and decide to back your idea or project.

Sean Olubodun is an entrepreneur who used Kickstarter to raise money for his business. He had some early success selling a few T-shirts with the image of his bulldog, Duke. He "bootstrapped" his business to start, but he used Kickstarter to raise money to expand.

Kickstarter has restrictions on what kinds of projects you can fund. But Indiegogo allows you to fund anything, and Crowdfunder focuses just on funding business. Be aware that these sites are up and running at the time this book is being written. These websites may have changed their focus or policies in the meantime. Or they could have vanished completely.

You can find other players in the crowd funding world and plenty of information about crowd funding options online. Each crowd funding site has its own rules and restrictions. My intent isn't to give you a full-blown analysis of crowd funding. But I want you to know that it could be a good option for funding your business.

Crowd funding may give you an advantage because the creativity of your idea and your pitch is as important as your content. In other words, you can pitch your business using a plan written on napkins. People willing to fund your project are going to look more at the merits of your idea. Unlike a bank, they won't make you crunch numbers on a spreadsheet.

I would have looked at crowd funding if it had been an option for me back when the traditional lenders were putting me through the wringer.

But there's also a downside to this freedom to bypass traditional "gatekeepers." You might get a half-baked business plan funded and then have a spectacular failure. Or you could struggle through some initial rough spots and damage your business reputation. Sometimes gatekeepers are helpful mentors. So it's a good idea to find a business mentor if you do choose the crowd funding route.

As a point of clarification: the crowd funding options I'm talking about here are what the SEC classifies as "cash donations." You offer an "incentive" for various levels of funding, but these are "contributors," not investors.

Peer Lending

A close relative of crowd funding is "peer lending." The two major players are Lending Club and Prosper. You can borrow up to $35,000 for any purpose you like. On the other side of your funding option are the investors who look at your proposal and decide how much they're willing to put in the hat.

When enough people buy in, your loan gets funded. These investors will probably want more of a traditional business plan than the crowd funding folks. After all, you'll be paying them interest and they'll want to see that you've got some strategy to be successful and pay them back. You can take a look online for peer-to-peer funding and find out if this is an option for you.

Keep in mind: the landscape for peer lending and crowd funding can change quickly. As I write this, I see Lending Club announced a few days ago they will now loan to small businesses who want to borrow $15,000 to $100,000. But books aren't as dynamic as other media. The information here may differ from what the peer lending world is like in the future.

Private Loans

Private loans are similar to peer lending, but instead of a lot of people loaning a little money, you've got a few (or one) loaning you all the money you need.

You may find "angel investors" who are looking for startup companies to invest in. These are people with money who are looking for alternatives to "traditional" investments. You'll pay them a higher interest rate than they can make elsewhere, and they give you access to money with fewer hoops to jump through than a bank requires.

I'll list "venture capital" lenders here as well, but usually they'll take longer to make decisions and may require oversight and/or ownership stakes in your business.

Private loans can also come from family or friends. Your family may even be eager to loan you money if they like you a lot. But go take a cold shower and then sit down for a serious talk with yourself before you go down that road.

What happens if your business fails and you can't pay your friends and family back? Or what happens if you're not as successful as you expected? What if you're making enough to maintain your business but don't make enough to pay your debt?

And then, think about how your relationship changes when you borrow money from someone. Now you've got this obligation between you and your family or friends that wasn't there before. Can you still hang out with them without your debt being the elephant in the room no one wants to talk about? Can you tell I think this may be a bad idea?

Don't get me wrong. I'm not saying to never borrow money from friends or relatives. Just remember that borrowing money from your family or friends is like dancing in a minefield.

Find a Partner

You could find someone with plenty of money to be your business partner. This may initially sound like a good idea. But if borrowing money from a friend or relative is like dancing in a minefield, then going into business with someone is like dancing on a tightrope stretched over a minefield. It can be done. Other people do it. But can you?

To cover all the ins and outs of having a partner in business would take a whole book in itself. I'm only going to give you a thumbnail sketch.

You need to at least consider doing the following if you're going to have a partnership: Sit down with your partner and hash out an agreement down to the tiniest imaginable detail. This isn't something to be done over a cup of coffee in an afternoon. Take time. Write everything down. Then go through it again to make sure you didn't miss something.

Edit what you've written and then write some more. Imagine everything that could possibly go wrong and talk about how you'll handle it. Talk about money and how it gets split up. Do your skills have the same value as your partner's? How will you judge the relative value of the skills you each bring to the party?

What happens if one of you wants to quit? Who's going to make decisions? If your partner's bringing money and you're bringing skills, what else is your partner going to contribute to running the business? Again, I'm not saying having a partner in business is a bad option. But you need to realize what you're getting into if you go down this road.

To be fair, you can find some advantages in a partnership. The right person with previous entrepreneurial experience could be the asset you need to shine. Just be sure to follow my advice and work out all the details before saying "I do" to a partner. (Yes, it's that kind of commitment.)

Bootstrapping

My wife worked at a copier dealership while I floundered through my first years in business. My start up costs and overhead were low. As such, I could have had success in my first year of business, had I known what I was doing. As it was, I made less than minimum wage.

You have an advantage I didn't. You have a formula to price your TT&P for profit. Even so, bootstrapping your business might be a struggle.

Bootstrapping your business may not work well if you need a large up-front investment for equipment or inventory. Also, it may not be good choice if your break-even point is a long way off. You see, money has an emotional component. Your spouse or partner may be a patient, loving and giving person. But your relationship can spiral into the abyss if you continually lose money in your business.

Decide What Will Work for You

Choosing how you fund your business is a major decision. I hope you've been practicing your decision-making skills. Take time and look at your funding options. I won't swear that this is an exhaustive list. You might find some kind of creative plan that suits you better. But do your own research on the benefits and drawbacks of funding your business. Then choose wisely.

In the next chapter I'll talk about keeping track of your money and your options for the legal structure of the business you'll put your money in.

Chapter 9

Manage Your Money

You've heard the "Don't put all your eggs in one basket" advice, haven't you? Financial advisers say it this way: "Diversify your investments."

You're going to do the exact opposite as an entrepreneur. You're putting everything you've got into your idea to create a business. What you need to do is this: "Put all your eggs in one basket, and then watch that basket!" Wisdom from the book of Proverbs advises you to keep a careful eye on the business that makes you money. Because it's easy for money to sprout wings, like an eagle, and fly away.

Watching your money is called "bookkeeping." Yes, I know this is basic and you've heard the term. What I want you to understand is you have to do it. I know lots of small business owners just throw all their receipts in a box. Then they spend days on end sorting through it at the end of the year.

I never waited a full year, but I've let piles of papers bury my desk before I did my bookkeeping tasks. And I put off enough of it to requires days of torture at the end of the year. So I speak from experience when I say, "Make time to keep your books."

Accounting Software

You can use pencil and paper for your bookkeeping. I rent space to store my utility trailer, and the owners keep accounts in a ledger book. I'll take a wild guess here. You're going to use a computer instead of paper and pencil. This brings me to my point: what bookkeeping software to use.

The 800-pound gorilla of bookkeeping software is a company called Intuit. Quicken is their personal money management program and Quickbooks is their business accounting software. You can find free bookkeeping programs and other companies who sell accounting packages. But Quickbooks is similar to Microsoft: almost everyone uses them.

I have a love/hate relationship with Quickbooks. I've tried other options, but I keep coming back.

One of the drawbacks of Quickbooks is its complexity. Translation: you'll spend a lot of time figuring out how to use it. Intuit has a small window for free customer support. I don't have proof, but I suspect they make more money on support and training to use their software than they do on selling it in the first place.

One reason I use it is because my accountant has Quickbooks, and I can just send my file to him at the end of the year. I've also been using it a long time and don't have to pay for ongoing support.

If you decide to go for freeware or options other than Quickbooks, be sure you can export to a different file format. You may change your mind and want to switch. You can also find "cloud" accounting software online. One such company I've looked at is Patriot Software. They charge a monthly fee, and you can choose from various options according to your needs. Such a company might be an option for you.

Whether it's an online software or a program like Quickbooks, you need to have accounting software to track your business.

Make a Line in the Sand

I'm repeating myself here again. I hope you've caught onto the fact that your personal money and business money need separate accounts. You've got a personal budget and a business budget.

I realize you might not have been really paying attention the first time, so I need to remind you. You'll need a separate bank account for your business.

And don't buy personal stuff from your business account. Now, even as I write this, I know you're going to ignore me and do it anyway. Only the most hidebound, check-off-every-box business owners NEVER buy personal stuff out of their business account. But don't make it a habit. Don't even do it once in a while. Do it RARELY. Keep your business stuff separated from your personal stuff.

Separating your business and personal money reminds you that your business is separate from you. Yes, you are the owner, but when you use business money to buy things for yourself, you can get in the habit of thinking of your business money as a "backup account" of money you can use. The danger of thinking this way is that you may forget some of the overhead expenses that money is supposed to cover.

Customers Pay You

Here's the way your business is supposed to work. You give your TT&P to your customers and they give you money. Sounds easy, right? But your business might be in an industry that's not so cut-and-dried.

For example, you will wait months to be paid if you're selling your TT&P to the government. The same goes when you sell your TT&P to a business. They usually expect you to give them a bill they can pay later, sometimes much later.

The people or businesses that owe you money are referred to as "Accounts Receivable." You don't want accounts receivable in your business if you can help it. And if you have to have accounts receivable, get these people to pay you as quickly as possible.

You'll be surprised how easy it is to get so caught up in selling, marketing, and running your business you neglect your accounts receivables.

I've mentioned cash flow earlier, but I didn't really explain it. Your money comes in from selling your TT&P. Your money goes out for your overhead. This is cash flow. Positive cash flow means the income is more than the out-go.

Accounts receivable can plug up your cash flow if you don't stay on top of them.

For some reason, the people you owe are more anxious for you to pay them than your *accounts receivables* are motivated to pay you. It's this exact situation entrepreneurs call a "cash flow problem." You don't want cash flow problems.

You Set the Terms

It's vital to determine up front how you expect to be paid. Attorneys receive a retainer: an up-front payment for legal service to be delivered. Receiving a deposit up front is common in construction as well as other industries. Payment upon delivery or completion of a service is the standard in others.

You will do well to remember the Golden Rule: He who has the gold makes the rules. It sucks worse than being an underpaid employee when you put out your best TT&P and then have someone else take their own sweet time to pay you.

If you don't know the norm for your area of business, do some research. Avoid accounts receivables if you can. Give the shortest payment terms possible if you're forced to have accounts receivables. You want cash to flow in as quickly as possible. Stay on top of your accounts. Don't let slow-paying customers turn into non-paying customers.

Income Taxes

Your personal budget has an innocent looking line called "income taxes." You also had this line on your paycheck as an employee. The government designated your employer to collect taxes from you. When you're self-employed you're responsible to pay your own taxes.

Here's good news and bad news. The good news: you have more deductions when you're self-employed. For example, you can deduct the business miles you drive. You can deduct part of your home as a home office. These are the good things.

The bad news: you now have to pay the other half of your social security and Medicaid, an extra 7% percent. If you didn't already know, your employer matches the money you pay to social security. When you're self-employed, the government counts you twice — once as the "employed" and once as the "self."

End-of-the-year tax preparation is about as fun as a trip to the dentist. Brace yourself. You'll have double the work when you're self-employed. You can't just look at your paycheck deductions or W2 form.

You have to subtract your business expenses from your business income. You pay taxes on the profit you made. Remember my advice to stay on top of your bookkeeping? It's no fun spending frantic days upon days sorting through piles of paper rushing to beat the deadline.

You may not have thought much about how your employer was a collection agent for the IRS. Your taxes were deducted from your paycheck, and you only worried about taxes once a year.

Well, the IRS doesn't want to wait that long. They want you to pay "quarterly estimated" payments. They even have a form — imagine that — to help you decide how much money to send them. It's the 1040-ES. You'll find "clear and understandable" instructions, as well as a worksheet, if you search the IRS website.

Now, you may say, "I'm not going to mess with this. I'll hire a bookkeeper." I understand. A good bookkeeper can be a great asset. He or she will free you up to do what you do best. I kind of imagine bookkeeping isn't what you do best.

But you will want to know how to do the bookkeeping yourself because you should always check the bookkeeper's work. Okay, I'm going to say that again in case you missed it. You should ALWAYS check over what your bookkeeper does before you send your money off to the government or anyone else. Remember, watch your money and your marketing like a lion watches a wildebeest.

So even if you hire a bookkeeper you still need to schedule time to review your expenses. And learn the ins and outs of how to read profit and loss reports and financial statements.

Find an Accountant

There's no reason to send the IRS any more money than you have to. I've mentioned accountants before, like I assumed you were going to have one in your pocket. I didn't have an accountant for my first several years of business. But then, I didn't really have a clue about running a business either. I did my own taxes and muddled my way through. It was really my only choice. I didn't have enough cash flow to hire an accountant.

But you're not going to have that problem, are you? Because I've told you how to price your TT&P, and you've already figured the cost of an accountant in your budget.

The "big box" tax services will claim they can handle your business taxes. Software companies promise "quick and easy" solutions for your small-business taxes as well. Can you tell I'm suspicious of these claims? Let me ask. Do you want some random guy quickly looking over your books and throwing out a number for the taxes you owe? Can a computer program find every deduction you might qualify for?

I think you'll be better off in the long run to find a real accountant, a CPA. A good accountant will save you more money than you spend on his or her service. A good accountant will advise you and help you plan your business strategies to save you money on your taxes.

Accountants range between two extremes: Bean Counter and Tax Ninja.

Accountants

Bean Counter — Tax Ninja

The IRS tax code is thousands of pages long. The tax code is designed to help certain people keep from paying taxes. And when you're one of the "certain people," you get to pay less too.

The Bean Counter accountants' primary aim is safety. Bean Counters avoid any shadow of doubt in the pages of the tax code. Their main focus is to avoid the risk of red flags or anything that might cause an audit.

They'll tell you you're not really one of the "certain people" these deductions were made for.

The Tax Ninja, on the other hand, lives to find deductions for you. Tax Ninjas believe you're in the "certain people" categories. They're fearless. They love to argue with the IRS if their clients are ever audited. They're creative thinkers, looking for even the most obscure loophole in the tax code. Tax Ninja accountants will save you a lot of money on your taxes, but you may risk an audit and have to defend your deductions. However, a good Tax Ninja will be fighting for you, so it's not as scary as you might imagine.

Figure out where you want to be on this continuum. Find an accountant that matches up to your level of comfort between Tax Ninja and Bean Counter. Talk to your network of people and ask for referrals. You may have to search hard if you're looking for a Tax Ninja. More accountants lean toward the Bean Counter side of the scale.

Also, ask for references when you interview accountants. And interview the clients they give as references. You're going to rely on your accountant for a vital part of your life — dealing with the IRS. You don't want any surprises, trust me. I speak from experience.

Business Structures:

A Thumbnail Sketch

Beyond taxes, your accountant can also advise you on business entities. Talk to your accountant about what kind of business structure you should have. He or she should be able to help you weigh the options about whether to be a sole proprietor or whether it makes sense for you to form a corporation or LLC.

Also, don't expect to interview accountants in the United States between January and April. They're a little busy then.

Sole Proprietor

A "sole proprietor" business is easy to start. You can just decide you're going to be in business and SHAZAM, you're a sole proprietor. You're a real business. You figure your deductions and your profits and then pay your taxes like every other business.

You'll file your profits on your personal income tax return using a form called "Schedule C." Figuring out Schedule C isn't much different from any of the other tax forms you use if you're doing your income taxes. You'll also have to include social security taxes under Schedule SE.

The tax preparation software claims to be able to handle these forms as well. The "big box" tax preparation companies also say they can do sole proprietors' taxes. It's true, you can probably handle taxes yourself or use tax software or a big-box tax service when you're only a sole-proprietor.

But one downside to being a sole proprietor is that you have no legal protection. You can be sued and held personally responsible if you have a major screw-up or if some crazy loon decides to make your life hell and sue you. You may be thinking, "I'm a good person. Who would want to sue me?" I know you're a good person and would never intentionally hurt anyone. But, accidents happen, no matter how careful you are.

Let me give you a real-life example. My regular drive took me past a home under construction. One morning, when it was almost finished, I drove by and the house was on fire. I later learned a painter left stain-soaked rags lying out. The rags spontaneously burst into flames. (That's why used stain-rags are supposed to be left in a closed metal container, in case you didn't know.)

I wasn't involved in this project at all, but here's what I do know. The painter was a sub-contractor, an independent business owner, working under the general contractor/builder. If the owners were so inclined, they could sue both the general contractor and painter (the sub-contractor) for damages. The painter would be personally liable as a sole-proprietor if his insurance didn't cover the lawsuit settlement.

The fire was real, in this case. The lawsuit was a "what-if" I added to make my point.

Now most people are reasonable and don't sue. Most people will work with you if problems or accidents happen. But some people run to a lawyer whenever something goes wrong. There are some crazy people out there. And there are equally hungry attorneys willing to file lawsuits for the crazies.

Partnerships

If you decide to have a partner in business (remember my warnings), you can set up a partnership as easily as a sole proprietor structure. You each file taxes as individuals, based on the profit each of you receive from the business.

I'm not an attorney and don't even play one on TV, so this isn't legal advice. In a partnership, both of you are fully responsible for all the taxes the business owes. The IRS will be knocking on your door if your partner doesn't pay. Any liability claims or lawsuit against one partner may carry over to the other.

Remember what I said about partnerships and dancing in a minefield?

Corporations

Protection from lawsuits is one of the primary benefits of doing business as a corporation. A corporation is a separate legal entity. It's like creating a virtual person, a virtual identity. A corporation isn't you. So a corporation protects you if a whacko tries to sue you. And if the whacko wins the lawsuit, he or she can only get the money that's in the corporation: your personal assets aren't at risk.

The down side for a regular corporation is that your income is taxed twice. The corporation is taxed when it makes money and then you're taxed when the corporation pays money to you as the owner. This type of corporation is called a "C-corporation."

You can, however, form an S-corporation. It gives you all the legal protection of a corporation, but the profits pass through to you as personal income, without being taxed twice.

To create a corporation, either "C" or "S," you file incorporation papers in your state and also apply for an employer identification number with the IRS. You can use a lawyer or an online incorporation service to do this. Yes, you can set up a corporation by yourself. But if you're really concerned about protecting yourself from liability, you're better off shopping for a good attorney to help.

LLC: Limited Liability Company

An LLC is kind of a hybrid between an S-corp and sole proprietor. You have the liability protection of a corporation without the formal structure of a corporation. Like a corporation, you have to file letters of organization in your state and get an employer identification number from the IRS. My accountant tells me you can also choose to be taxed in the same way as an S-corp, which offers a definite advantage and cost savings.

One reason I say you're better off finding a real accountant is because he or she should be able to advise you on what business structure is best for you. Your accountant will be dealing with your business year to year. Talk to him or her first. Then talk to a lawyer, if you decide you need one, to set up a business entity. Your accountant may have a referral for an attorney who can do a good job for a fair price. Remember to interview your lawyer like you did your accountant. Make sure he or she can give you the results you want.

Insurance

Your risk of a lawsuit is probably low. But your odds are greater than the odds of you winning the lottery . . . I guess getting sued would be a kind of reverse lottery. Even so, make sure you have liability insurance for whatever you do in your business. If you're a consultant, Realtor, or even a life coach, your liability is more in line with what they call "errors and omission" insurance.

I'd suggest you buy more liability coverage if you're a sole proprietor. Your risk is more. And make sure you understand the coverage. You don't want to find out after the fact that some of the stuff you do in your business isn't covered.

Do a yearly review of your coverage to be sure you're up to date. It was during a yearly review that I discovered a hole in our insurance coverage. Our policy didn't cover clients' property if we took it to our shop, a standard practice for us. We never had a claim, but I'm glad I found and closed that loophole.

Chapter Wrap-up

You can buy complete books on subjects I've brushed by here in a paragraph or two. I know I mashed together two topics wrapped with one slender thread: each one relates to money. You need to keep track of your cash flow. And you need to choose the business structure that is best for you to use to make your money.

My goal is to point you to decisions you'll need to make in order to start your own unique business. There's no way I could cram a book with information for every possible business.

I hope your wheels are turning by now. I hope ideas are flowing and a plan for your business is taking shape. If so, you might be an entrepreneur.

Chapter 10

Contain and Control

I know what you've heard. But they lied. You can't *manage* time. Yes, I know you've been to seminars. Your boss may have told you to read time management books. I don't care what you've been told by those other guys, the productivity gurus. Time is unmanageable.

Just stop and think for a minute. What do the words "time management" really mean? You are in charge when you manage something. You set the guidelines. You make the rules.

Time ignores you. You can't "save" time. You can't "make" time. You can't "manage" time. Time is a constant. You can't store it. You can't produce more of it. You get the same amount of time as everyone else does.

So why am I making a big deal about "time management"? It's because words mean things, and the words you use influence how you think. I know you know better, but when you talk about how to "manage" time there's a part of you that ends up thinking of it as a commodity rather than a constant.

For example, you can "manage" your money to get more of it. When you speak of managing your money it's more than budgeting. You're also talking about putting your money out there in some kind of investment and you expect it to multiply.

You feel a degree of control over your money when you "manage" it. Likewise, when you talk about "managing" time, you tend to *feel* as if time and money submit to similar rules. Just think about trying to have control over your time exactly like you have control over your money and see how far you get.

Are you with me on this? You don't control your time; you only control the decisions you make as you go through time. That is, you control your schedule. So rather than "managing time" what you really do is budget time.

You see, you can budget both your time and your money. You can spend both your time and your money. You can even talk about investing your time and your money. But here's where the similarity breaks down. You invest your money to get more money. You don't get more time when you invest your time.

Decisions in Time

A teacher had a gallon jar on the table and filled it with large rocks. Then he said, "Is the jar full?"

"Yes," the students answered.

The teacher then took small rocks and shook the jar so they settled in the spaces between the big rocks.

"Is the jar full?" the teacher asked.

"Yes," said the students.

The teacher took sand and put in the jar and shook it so the sand filled the spaces between the little rocks.

"Is the jar full now?" asked the teacher.

The students by now were catching on. So they said, "No. The jar isn't full."

The teacher then poured water in slowly until it filled the remaining space and the jar was full.

"What's the lesson here?" the teacher asked.

"There's always room for just a little more," said one student.

"No," replied the teacher. "The lesson is, if you don't put the big rocks in first you'll never get them to fit."

Your Full Jar

You will live out the meaning of this lesson every day when you're self-employed. Each day will bring you more to do than will ever fit in your jar. Someone once said you can be successful at being self-employed by working half-days. You just pick what 12 hours you want to work and go to it.

In reality, you might find this statement to be a lie. Working 12 hours a day may not come close to being enough. You'll start looking for an Einstein-level physicist to help you create wormholes in time. Or maybe you'll want to clone yourself like Michael Keaton in the movie *Multiplicity*.

Keep 'Em Spinning

Have you ever seen anyone demonstrate plate spinning? The performer puts plates on top of flexible rods and starts them spinning. The performer races franticly from plate to plate to keep the spinning plates from slowing down and falling off. If you haven't ever seen plate spinning, look up the Erich Brenn clip from the Ed Sullivan show on YouTube.

Plate spinning is a good illustration of what being self-employed feels like. Whatever thing you're doing right this minute, you've also got those other plates spinning across the room. And they're going to fall unless you get to them in time.

When you're self-employed, whatever you're working on needs your full concentration. But in the back of your mind, you're thinking about all those other plates across the room, spinning slower and slower. And you know you've got to get there before they shatter on the floor.

So you end up hurrying through the thing you're working on, cutting corners and "half-assing" it. And then when you go to the other spinning plate, you're thinking about that thing you were doing before, that thing that needs to be tweaked and you really need to go back and make it good enough. So the new thing you're doing now gets half-assed as well.

So it goes until it seems like everything you've done is half-assed. And you're worn out because you've still got to keep all the plates spinning.

You wanted to be self-employed so you can be your own boss. But your boss has turned into a raving maniac.

The time management gurus tell about the rocks in the jar and gently say, "Put the big rocks in first," waving their hand like a Jedi mind master. I look up and say, "Well, excuse me! All my rocks look like big rocks!"

Shrink Your Rocks

You can't make the jar bigger. You only get 24 hours in your day. So your only choice is to make some of your rocks smaller. Now don't look at me like I've grown two heads. You can really do this.

Remember in school how you'd have days or weeks to write a paper or study for a test? You'd start your research or study at an easy pace with no worries . . . you've got plenty of time. But you always ended up cramming at the last minute to finish the paper or study for your test. I know you did, at least once.

Suppose, instead, the teacher only gave you two days to start with? You'd be upset. You'd think it was unfair. But you could still do the same work in a shorter deadline. You were doing it anyway, but you were just procrastinating beforehand. Your project expanded to fill the time allotted. So the work you could really do in two days ends up lasting two weeks.

I've heard it explained like this: Any project will expand to fill the time allotted for it.

So to keep this tendency of "project bloat" from sabotaging you as an entrepreneur, you need to be able to sort your rocks before you drop them in your jar. Some of the things on your to-do list look bigger than they need to be. (Remember what I said about your school assignments.)

On the other hand, some of the things on your list look easy, but they will mushroom to gigantic size before you know it. And some of the stuff you can just drop off the list for now. I know you think you need to do these things, but the world won't end if you drop them. There's nothing quite as frustrating as busting your butt all day and then realizing you've been working on stuff that really wasn't all that important.

Pick Your System

Look up "time management" in Wikipedia and you'll find a list of methods you can use to prioritize your tasks. I'm only going to talk about one of them here because it's a way to illustrate what this chapter is about. The Eisenhower Matrix is a method that helped me prioritize the demands for my time. The Eisenhower Matrix looks like this:

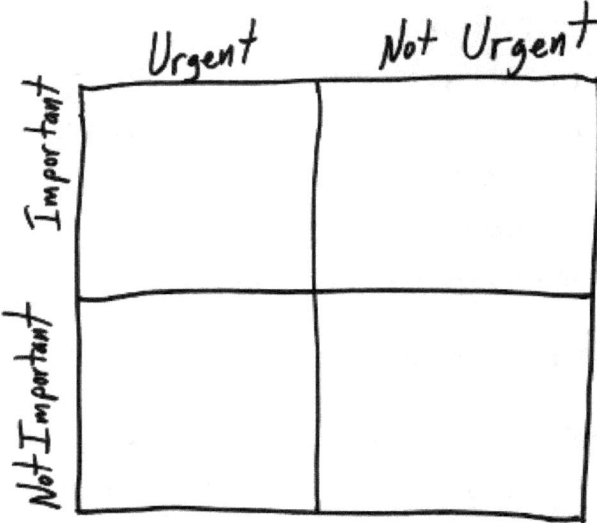

The quadrants represent a matrix you can use to sort your to-do list. You need to see that the important stuff gets done and the really important stuff doesn't get neglected.

The tasks you encounter each day will fall into one of these four categories.

Important / Urgent

This category is for things that have to be taken care of NOW. You've probably at one time or another described a hectic day as "putting out fires." You're going to have plenty of fires burning when you're self-employed. Everything feels like a fire when you start your business. All of it is important. It all has to be done right away.

Sort these "fire" projects from biggest to smallest. Take care of the biggest ones first. (Just like the rocks.) The trick is to make sure nothing slips into this category from the next one on the list: the things that aren't important but feel urgent.

Not Important / Urgent

These are tasks or projects that feel like they have to be done right now. But when nothing serious happens to you if they don't get done right away, put them in this category. I'm talking about things like talking to the salesperson on the phone and all the interruptions that feel urgent. They pop up demanding to be done right now. But they're lying to you. They can wait.

You can recognize the Not Important tasks when you ask yourself, "What happens if this doesn't get done right now?" or "What happens if this doesn't get done at all?" If the answer is, "Nothing," or "Nothing serious," then don't do it now. Put it off.

Now, don't get me wrong. Many of these tasks can't be simply forgotten. They are like ticking timers on bombs strapped to a gas can. If you ignore the deadline to complete these tasks you'll have a fire on your hands. So you put them off and schedule them to be done when they are both urgent and important.

Not Important / Not Urgent

You encounter lots of things you can do each day that aren't all that important and have no deadline. Activities like playing video games, surfing the Internet, checking Facebook can suck you in and sidetrack you.

These are the time-wasters you do when you know you should be doing something more important.

There's something in each of us that seduces us into the quicksand of wasted time. The insidious thing about these time-wasters is that you rationalize: you tell yourself you need a *little* break. You tell yourself you'll get busy with real work in just a minute. But right now, you deserve this little distraction.

And before you know it you're blown completely off course with nothing to show for all the time you just spent. The thing is that piddling around with distractions makes you feel tired rather than rested. You feel tired because you *feel* as if you were working.

Now don't get me wrong. You need to take a break from working all the time. Remember, we're talking about how to move yourself through time without driving yourself crazy. You need time in each quadrant of this matrix. But my experience is that I need to fight to keep the Important/Urgent and the Not Important/Not Urgent tasks from totally consuming my time budget.

Important / Not Urgent

The most important elements of your life reside in this quadrant of the Eisenhower Matrix. These are your family, your friends and your physical, emotional and spiritual health. Jesus once asked a question about the important things in life that goes like this: "What good is it if you gain the whole world but lose your soul?" In other words, what good is it to be successful in business if you lose the people you love and turn into the person you hate?

The Important / Not Urgent items are easily ignored. You may not see a ticking timer on these activities. But just because you don't see it doesn't mean there's no timer there. These things are Important. You can put them off for a while, but ignore them at your peril.

Ignore your health and it will eventually deteriorate to the point that's all you'll be able to think about. Ignore the people you love most, you'll end up alone and miserable. What good is it to be successful in business and lose your soul?

Walking Through Fire

It's all nice and cozy to sit here and think about budgeting your time. You can smile and nod and vow you'll balance all your tasks in harmony. Birds will sing. Flowers will bloom. You'll have everything under control, you think. You'll know differently when you launch your business.

To mash up the metaphors I've given you so far, you're going to feel like everything in your business is a spinning plate, a big rock, and a raging fire. There's really no avoiding it either. You'll have a ton of new things to learn, and fast.

Decisions you didn't even know you had to make will fly in under the radar as a sneak attack. Everything has to be done NOW! Don't panic. Yes, you're going to feel overwhelmed. But you'll survive.

A saying I learned long ago: When you're up to your ass in alligators, it's hard to remember your original intent was to drain the swamp. You need to keep your wits about you and stay focused.

You can't survive long-term in the frantic got-to-get-it-all-done-now mode. Once you get things under some kind of control in your business, you need to go back to the Eisenhower Matrix and get control of your time budget.

It took me way too long to figure out my priorities were out of whack. I spent all my time fighting fires and distracting myself with non-important-non-urgent nonsense. I became exhausted physically, emotionally and spiritually.

You Need Boundaries

"Self-employed" is made up of two words connected with a dash. What happens, however, is you end up feeling like you're *selfemployed.* Your personal identity merges with your business. Of course, you are your business when you're self-employed. You do the work. You make the decisions. You promote your business by promoting yourself. After a while, the line between "self" and "employed" evaporates. Your business consumes more of you as it grows. Your business becomes like the Borg in Star Trek: "You will be assimilated."

You're even more likely to be swallowed up by your business when you're a home-based business because it claims space in your home. I know it sounds as if I'm stating the obvious . . . a home-based business is, by definition, in your home. But a home-based business is like the camel's nose in the tent. It slowly creeps in, to take more of your home.

Your business lurks in the corners, waiting for you as soon as you wake up. You tell yourself, "I've got this one little thing to take care of," and four other things creep out of the shadows, demanding your attention. Before you know it, a couple of hours have passed and you realize you've been swallowed whole once again. Soon you find yourself always working. You're checking your email while you brush your teeth.

Max Headroom

The physical space your home-based business takes is an issue. But the mental and emotional space is a more difficult issue. Your business can take over the space in your head whether it's located in your home or elsewhere.

You have appointments to keep track of. You have the Fires to get under control. The past customer calling with a problem. The worry about whether you'll have enough business coming in three weeks from now. Remembering the deadline for your quarterly taxes. Thinking of creative and effective marketing ideas. And the list goes on.

"Resistance is futile. You will be assimilated."

I've been fortunate to meet several life coaches. They all tell me I need boundaries. You need to get back that line — that dash — inserted back between yourself and your business. You get back to being self-employed.

Drawing boundaries between your business and yourself isn't easy. You tend to draw them in pencil rather than using a Sharpie. And how do you tame the voices in your head? You tell yourself, "Just one little thing to take care of," and before you know it you're sucked in again.

You can use lots of different strategies to make boundaries for yourself. So what I'm about to tell you isn't the end-all solution. These are the things that worked for me. I hope they connect with you. But if they don't, keep looking and trying until you get something that works for you. The important thing is to know resistance is not futile. You've got to fight against being assimilated by your business.

First of all, get serious about this. Don't just sit there and smile and nod to make me feel better. I know you're thinking, "Oh, yeah. I need to remember this. I'll get around to it. Set boundaries, check." No, I'm leaning across the table and looking you in the eye. This is important! You've got to pay attention here.

See This Line!

Start by drawing boundaries in your head. The cool thing about being self-employed is that you are your business. The bad thing about being self-employed is that you are your business. Your business lives in your head. It wakes you up at night. It's all you think about.

You draw boundaries in your head by setting time when you are not working. Stop right now and read that again. In your mind, draw a line in the sand. Stare down your pile of work and say, "You're not crossing this line."

If you're a list maker and schedule keeper, write it down. If you're a "go-with-the-flow" free spirit, make it a promise to yourself. And when the time comes for not working, DON'T BE WORKING. Don't be thinking of all the things you have to do. Don't be thinking of work at all. Be thinking of anything besides work. Picture this exercise as a mental Whack-a-Mole. You hold the mallet in your mind and when work thoughts pop up you smack them back down. Believe me, this is a game you need to win.

Carrying your business in your head means you're never "off the clock." You can do it for a while, but eventually it will wear you down. So create space in your schedule and tell your brain to be quiet and quit working for a while. That is, to quit working on business. You don't want your brain to completely shut down. That would be awkward.

Work When You're Working

Drawing a boundary in your head also means that you WORK when it's time to work. Being your own boss means YOU'RE THE BOSS. It's easy to get distracted by personal stuff when supposed to be working. And the same way you carry work stuff in your head while you're "not working" you carry personal stuff in your head when you're supposed to be working.

Of course, you've always done this, even when you were employed. But when you're an employee and everyone is standing around talking about the latest American Idol contest your boss comes by and tells you to get back to work. Now that you're the boss, you'll have to tell yourself to get back to work.

Border Crossing: Passport Please!

You will occasionally have to let something important cross your boundary. But make those times the exception, not the rule. Remember, part of the reason you wanted to be self-employed was to have more say-so in how you live your life. Don't let work bully its way into your personal space. Don't let personal stuff encroach into your work. Work when you work, and don't work when you don't. But be flexible enough to make exceptions when you have to.

Physical Boundaries at Home

The physical boundaries you create for your home-based business are just as important as your mental boundaries. Designate a space for your business to live in your home. Use it for business. Resist the temptation to drag your work out on the living room couch while you watch TV. Don't leave work in piles on the dining room table.

I realize you may not have room to spare. You may have to work from your kitchen table. If this is your situation, find a way to store your work somewhere else so your work doesn't live in your living space. Work when you're working and then pack it up and put it away when you're not working.

You're probably thinking, "What a hassle." Of course it's a hassle. But, believe me, you really need to have your own living space. Keep your business in a separate space so it's out of sight. The lines you draw in your head are easier to maintain if your business isn't constantly living in your personal space.

Make strong boundaries at first, concrete and barbed wire. You can relax them later as needed. It's harder to start off squishy and try to tame a monster later.

Set these boundaries in your physical space and "in your head space" before you even start your business. Don't wait until you're five years in and about to have a nervous breakdown. Defeat Godzilla before he grows up. Don't wait until he's knocking over skyscrapers.

Translate Your Time Management Language

You've probably dealt with all this "time management" stuff as an employee. I can almost hear you yawning as you say, "I know all this. Been to the seminar. Got the tee-shirt." But when you become an entrepreneur, the demands on your time and attention intensify. The strategies you used as an employee might not work any more.

You may have had a demanding boss as an employee, but you could still shut the door or hang up the phone or walk away and not have to deal with him or her for a while. You could even sneak some time at work to watch cat videos online.

But when you're self-employed, you can't hide from your boss. You can't shut the door or hang up the phone. The voice in your head will keep demanding and nagging. So make your plan now. Know when to tell your boss-self to back off and give you space.

You can't escape the fact that your business is you you're self-employed. You need to make sure that you don't become your business.

You have 24 hours every day. Remember, you don't control the hours. You control yourself. You also control and contain the space, mental and physical, your business occupies. The decisions you make minute by minute and hour by hour add up to what you get out of your life, for good or bad. Choose well.

Chapter 11

The Powers That Be

Someone in the crowd asks, "Rabbi, is there a proper blessing for the Czar?" The Rabbi looks down and strokes his beard. He slyly smiles, lifts his head and says, "May the Lord bless and keep the Czar . . . far away from us."

As a small business owner, you will relate to this scene from Fiddler on the Roof. You'll feel the government's hand on your business no matter what kind of business you have. The rules of the game vary for each level of government and the location of your business. At the least you'll have paperwork, fees and hoops to jump through. You may have restrictions and roadblocks as well.

Your Local Government

Let's start out close to home. Your city government will likely require you to get a business license. Yes, even a home-based business will require a license. You'll have to pay a fee each year and abide by the city's zoning and sign regulations.

Your business may have regular inspections from government agencies. Places such as restaurants and catering businesses have to be approved by the health inspector, for example. You may have other permits or use restrictions on how and where you can do business, depending on the city in which you live.

Home associations may also have rules and/or prohibitions for having a business in your home. So be sure to clear your plans with the "powers that be" in your backyard first. A call to your local Chamber of Commerce should get you headed in the right direction.

Courtesy Goes A Long Way

If you're thinking about starting a home-based business, make sure you do your best to be a good neighbor. Customers coming and going all day or employees' cars parked on the street will irritate even the most patient neighbors. Some cities have regulations against a retail-type business from your home, that is selling products or serving customers in your house. But even if your city allows this kind of home-based business, you don't want your neighbors making a call to the city zoning board and complaining, even if you're doing everything by the book.

The County

Your county government is the next level up in the government food chain. These are the guys that tax your house, your car, your boat and other kinds of personal property. Taxable personal property varies by state.

Most counties tax real estate, so if you own a business building you'll be paying taxes on that. But your personal property may also be taxed if you use it for business. More to the point, the county will tax your personal property as "business equipment." That is, once you use it as part of your business, it is not considered "personal" property any more. Now it's "business equipment" and subject to tax.

For example, suppose you're going to start a lawn-mowing business. You have a lawn mower, a trailer, an edge trimmer and yard tools. You're good to go. All this equipment is personal property.

But once you use your personal property in your business the county may tax it. Again, the rules will vary from state to state and county to county, but this tax can sneak up and surprise you. I was certainly surprised when the county assessors informed me the tools I'd owned for years were now subject to tax, and please send the money now.

Your State Government

Your state government is the next level up. Again, laws and regulations vary from state to state, and some states are friendlier to small businesses than others. Your state may require a license for the kind of work you do.

For example, some states license house painters and interior designers and every trade involved in house construction or remodeling. Other states only license general contractors--the ones who hire and manage subcontractors doing the actual work. Hairdressers and barbers usually have to have a state license. You might also be required to take continuing education classes to maintain your license.

It will be worth your while to keep up with your state laws and regulations that affect your industry. Sometimes rules change. The state of Kansas tried to clamp down on a business called "The Braidin' Maidens." These ladies went to events like the local Renaissance Festival and sold their services to braid hair. The state claimed that since they were working with another person's hair, even though they weren't cutting or coloring it, they would be required to hold cosmetology licenses.

The Bradin' Maidens won their case in court and were able to resume their business, but they were out of business until the case was resolved. Now, from what I read about the lawsuit, the Braidin' Maidens' business wasn't a full-time, bring-home-the-bacon business. They only worked a few weeks a year at the Renaissance Festival.

But imagine starting your business intending to make a profit only to have some state bureaucrats shut you down, forcing you to go to court to defend your livelihood. Like I said, you should be aware of both present and potential regulations your state requires in your business.

Corporations and LLCs

Your state government registers your business if you decide to do business as a corporation or LLC rather than a sole proprietor. Your state has rules and guidelines for corporations and LLCs. These rules and guidelines vary from state to state. You should find the information about setting up corporations and LLCs on your state's official website, usually in the Secretary of State's section.

You May Be An Employee

I was shocked when I found out the state wanted unemployment tax from me as the owner of my corporation. Technically, the corporation pays me a salary. The state considers it subject to unemployment taxes.

I asked if I could fire myself and collect unemployment. They chuckled and said, "No. You're the owner." I asked, "Then why do I have to pay?" They told me, "That's just the way it is." I grumble under my breath each time I pay this tax. And another thing: when you're an S-corp the federal government wants unemployment tax from your salary as well.

Are Your Sales Taxable?

Check with your state to find out if they tax your sales. If so, you need to register for a sales tax ID number. Sales tax laws also vary from state to state. They are also subject to change, so pay attention to what your state legislators are up to. For example, some states have no sales tax on grocery items. The state I live in doesn't tax labor on residential construction. Nor do they tax labor for hair stylists.

Most states have a list of products or services exempt from sales tax. But remember, the list of exemptions is always subject to change. So check your state's website — it's usually under the Department of Revenue — and see whether you TT&P is subject to sales tax. It doesn't hurt to give them a call as well and ask for specifics about your particular business.

State and Local Income Tax

And don't forget, your state and city may require you to send quarterly income tax estimated payments. Most states aren't as heavy-handed as the IRS about collections. You may be able to pay your state and local income tax at the end of the tax year. But it's still a good idea to pay your state and local taxes on a quarterly basis at least. Remember the Rabbi's blessing and keep the Czar far away from us.

The Federal Government

Now we come to the 800-pound gorilla: the federal government. Of course you know you'll be dealing with the IRS. You'll pay taxes on your profits. You'll also pay Social Security and Medicare taxes: and remember, they're double for self-employed.

If you decide to do business as an S-corp or LLC you'll need to register for an employer identification number (EIN). It can be a bit confusing. You set up a corporation or LLC at the state level, and then you register your business with the federal government to get an EIN. Think of it this way: your corporation or LLC is a virtual person. The EIN is the virtual person's social security number.

Typically you only have the IRS and taxes to deal with at the federal government level. But you can have snags and roadblocks from other federal agencies too. You may remember news stories of some business blocked from expanding because the EPA found an endangered species nearby. You may think your business is so small that the feds will surely never notice you. But you can still be impacted.

EPA: Get the Lead Out

Take, for example, the thousands of real estate investors renovating old homes. Real estate investors were on the front lines of pulling the United States out of the mortgage and housing crisis.

Foreclosed homes sit vacant and deteriorate to the point that only investors can buy them. Homeowners can't buy these homes because banks won't loan money on a derelict. Investors buy, rehab and then resell them. They make a profit, and people who buy or rent from them get a good home.

But a few years ago the EPA instituted new "lead paint" regulations: anyone working on pre-1978 houses was required to be "Lead Paint Certified." Real estate investors and remodeling contractors got squeezed because the EPA imposed their "regulations" almost overnight. And they laid on heavy fines — over $30,000 a day — for anyone caught working on a pre-1978 home without being certified.

Now don't get me wrong. Lead paint is a serious health risk. But the EPA mandated these changes and high penalties so quickly that few contractors were able to get certified in time. And the new rules push up the cost of doing business for contractors. The actual added cost the contractors have to bear is at least triple what the EPA estimates in their guidelines.

Some contractors and investors went out of business as a result. Others now refuse to work on houses built before 1978. And those contractors who do work on older homes raised their prices. So people who own older homes have to pay more. And investors have to charge more when they re-sell or charge higher rents.

The EPA and other government agencies could have a lot to say about how or whether you conduct your business. And the rules can change depending on the political climate of the day. It pays to be aware of the rules and shifting winds of bureaucracy rather than getting snared in a crackdown.

Roll With the Changes

Now you may be asking, "What's this have to do with me? I'm not a real estate investor or contractor." I told this story to illustrate how easy it is for your business to be impacted too. You'll have very few options if you end up on the other side of some federal agency and their regulations. Keep in mind that being a small business gives you some flexibility. You can adapt to changes in the government landscape if you must.

So research the federal regulations your business may have to follow. There may be some you don't know about yet. If you do get sideways with some federal agency by accident or through ignorance they won't give you a pass. They will assume you should have known better.

Sure Things

You've heard the saying that there are only two sure things in life: death and taxes. Of course you're there thinking there's more than just two — the sun coming up tomorrow, for instance. But I digress. My point is you're sure going to pay taxes when you make money. I know that you may have some friend of a friend who works for cash, never reporting income to the IRS.

Yes, some people work for cash and just put it in their pocket. Cash business doesn't leave a paper trail.

They figure the IRS will never know. Some estimate this "underground economy" accounts for two trillion dollars each year. If these figures are accurate, it's obvious there are a lot of people getting away with working for cash.

Don't be tempted to join this "underground economy." You might get away with taking cash under the table for a while. I know small business owners who have gotten away with it for years. But every so often you'll hear about a business owner who gets caught and has to pay tens of thousands of dollars in back taxes and penalties.

The IRS considers this tax fraud and you can end up in jail as well. The IRS has ways to find you if you try to hide your cash sales. For example, they offer a bounty to anyone willing to turn you in. The informant gets half of whatever the IRS collects in unpaid taxes. So you might not be as safe as you think when people pay you in cash.

Do the Right Thing

There are deeper issues here than just getting caught and paying a fine. You probably consider yourself honest and trustworthy. As such, your honesty should show up in all parts of your business, especially paying your taxes.

I may think the government is a bloated, wasteful, power-hungry bunch of political hacks who spend money like drunken sailors. But I'm not much different than those dishonest politicians if I take cash payments under the table. Do this, keep your books honestly and report all your income. Do it because it's the right thing to do.

Avoid Taxes, Legally

You can afford to do the right thing because you'll have legal ways to cut your taxes. You have more deductions as a business owner than you ever had as an employee. Find a tax-ninja accountant and you can legally save thousands of dollars on your taxes.

The US tax code is thousands of pages long and filled with wherefores, therefores and what-fors. The tax code is massive and complex so the wealthy can run their businesses and invest their money while avoiding taxes. When you become a business owner, you have access to some of these same deductions and tax breaks, even if you're not wealthy yet.

Businesses Don't Pay Taxes

And consider this fact: at the end of the day, businesses don't pay taxes. People pay taxes. Remember the personal and business budget you figured back in

Chapter Two? All of the expense from your not-so-silent partner — the government — get added to your budget and passed on to your customers. Taxes are part of your overhead. And, yes, every business does their budget this way.

That's why I say that businesses don't really pay taxes. Every tax increase on business is only an increase in their overhead passed on to you and me in the prices we pay. So if you're running your business the way you should you don't really need to be dishonest and cheat on your income by taking cash "under the table."

Keep your books clean and concentrate on growing your business. Taxes and the cost of whatever regulations the Czars of government slap on you are part of your overhead. Take some time and check out how much the "powers that be" will demand. Then make sure you've got it covered in your budget and move on. You've got a business to get up and running.

Chapter 12

Bring Your A-Game

"Eighty percent of life is showing up." - Woody Allen

I say, "Yes," to Woody Allen. And I'll add that you can be 90% of the way to success in business if you show up and also bring your A-game.

Your A-game is what we commonly call "customer service." You tend to remember good customer service because bad service seems to be so easy to find. Some companies treat you as if you're a nuisance, rather than the reason they're in business.

But stop for a minute and think about those companies. The entrepreneur who started the business didn't set out to create it as a place to ignore and abuse people. I'm sure the founder had good intentions, to provide a good product or service. Of course, you can get poor service from a small business as well. It's easier to pick on the big corporations with call centers on the other side of the world.

It Can Happen to You

I can hear you sitting there saying, "Not me. I'll never let poor service creep into my business." But don't fool yourself. You can get so busy keeping all the plates spinning that you forget the core of your business: serving your customer.

You let little things slip. An appointment gets missed. Phone calls don't get returned. You over-promise because you're trying to keep your customers happy. Your best intentions careen off the cliff.

Show Up and Bring Your A-Game

So what does your A-game look like? Well, it depends on your business. What do your customers expect from you? What kind of experience do they want when they do business with you? What frustrations do they have with other people in your industry — your competitors?

Find out what your customers expect. Then figure out how to give them all of that, plus something over the top they didn't expect. Make them say, "Wow!"

But wait, you're not finished yet. Get inside their head. Learn the things they want but don't yet know that they want. They'll think you're a genius if you can hit that spot.

In short, discover how you can serve your customers so well they'll love you for life.

Be Memorable

All the stuff I've thrown at you so far might be overwhelming. But hang in here with me on this. Your success depends on how well you serve your customers.

Your satisfied customers will go on their merry way and soon forget you. Give customers what they expect and they will be satisfied. You don't want satisfied customers. You want raving fans. Raving fans remember you. Raving fans will gush about you whenever they have a conversation that turns to what you do: your TT&P.

Now even with your best efforts, you're not going to make everyone into a raving fan. You won't make some customers happy no matter what you do. But you're not bringing your A-game if you only average three-star reviews.

Remember, your goal is to create Advocates: people who are happy to refer you and who want to refer you. The way you create Advocates on your A-list is to go all out. Give your customers way more than they expect.

The Spice Monger

I buy spices from our local farmer's market. Tables overflow with bags full of every spice imaginable. Each bag contains a small scoop, planted deep, handle up. My mouth waters as I wait. The mingled fragrances bring to mind hearty plates of savory food. The spice monger charges anywhere from two to four dollars per scoop, depending on the spice.

But when you place your order, he puts a scoop and a half in your bag. Understand that the posted price is a fantastic deal: less than half the price of buying from the grocery store. But he still gives more than he promises.

That extra half-scoop is what draws me back to his table instead of visiting the other spice monger down the aisle. Now I'm sure his price covers the scoop-and-a-half I get. But the price per scoop sets an expectation for me. So I always feel as if I'm getting extra, even though it's his standard procedure.

Do it on Purpose

This is important. Bringing your A-game isn't something you want to do by accident. Think about how you interact with your customers, from their first contact with you clear up until you've delivered the goods. Be like the spice monger. Create a plan and a system to set your customer's level of expectation and then deliver more than you promise.

When I say, "create a plan," I don't mean to just think about it and keep it in your head. Get a piece of paper, or go to your stack of napkins. Write your ideas down. Getting your ideas out of your head and onto something else will bring out stuff you never knew was in there.

Make an outline or draw circles, lines and arrows, whatever works best for you. Just make the time to put together a concrete plan for how you can serve your customers with excellence. This should be part of your business plan.

What Do Your Customers Want?

Think about how your customers will first contact you. Will it be by phone? By email? By text? How quickly will they expect a reply? Will they expect a live person to answer the phone if they call? How soon will they expect a return call if they leave a voicemail?

How soon will they expect an email response? Will they expect an instant response if they text? The answer will vary depending on the kind of business you have and the customers you serve. Baby boomers will be pleasantly surprised by a live voice answering the phone. Gen-Y and Millennials may not want to call you but will be happy to text or email.

If you have a business location with customers just walking in, think about what they expect when they come in the door. Do they want someone to greet them, or would they rather come in and browse first and not be bothered? Will your customers need help deciding what to buy, or can they just select what they want and take it to the checkout to buy it?

There's a fast-food restaurant in my area that used to yell out a greeting when people walked in the door, "Welcome to Moe's!" They stand out from the other fast-food places, with employees who sometimes act as if they're imparting a favor just to take your order.

You've heard the saying, "You only get one chance to make a first impression." Your customer's first impression starts when they contact you with the idea they might do business with you.

Your customer should already have a first impression about you from your marketing. Remember, your marketing is supposed to make you look good. So, when a potential customer contacts you, he or she should already expect you to be wonderful. Their first point of contact needs to confirm your awesomeness and leads them to an experience that transforms them from customer into a raving fan.

Selling Is Serving

Your A-game shows up in your sales process. You're selling from the first contact you have with your customer. You're selling while you do the work or deliver your TT&P. You're selling up until you get paid. Yes, being an entrepreneur in business means you have to sell.

But it's not like you think. Don't think of sales like the slick talker, selling ice to Eskimos. Sure, you can sell with high-pressure tactics. If you're pushy and annoying enough, people will buy from you just to get you to shut up and go away. But high-pressure sales tactics don't result in loyal, raving fans.

We're talking about A-game customer service. And selling is serving. When you sell, you help your customers make a decision that's in their best interest. You're not working in your customer's best interest if you're convincing them to buy from you just so you can make a sale. High-pressure sales tactics don't serve your customer and don't result in raving fans.

Find out what your customer wants and their motivation to buy it. Remember, people buy the things they want, not the things they need. Determine whether you can give them what they want and make them satisfied. Then find a way to deliver more than you promise, so customers walk away ecstatic.

Ask First, Then Tell

This means your sales process begins by asking questions of your prospective customer. Now, if they're interested in what you have to offer, they're going to start asking questions back. Don't be lured in and launch into a spiel about your product or service. Talk about yourself and what you can do for them, but stop and ask them questions.

Make sure you listen closely to the answers they give. Then ask more questions to get to the core of what they want. Your primary goal is to make your customer feel important. Make your customer believe you're going to do whatever it takes to help them get what they want or fix their problem. Because you're bringing your A-game, that's just what you'll do.

Your A-Game Means a Fine Presentation

Remember when we talked about marketing? The difference between being ordinary and super is all in the presentation. In the same way, your selling doesn't end when your customer says "Yes." Deliver your TT&P with a good presentation. Impress them. Make them feel like they made a good decision to buy from you.

Imagine going to a restaurant for dinner. You see tasteful decor. The lighting is soft, but adequate. The hostess greets you and shows you to a table. The silverware is wrapped in cloth napkins. The waiter describes the specials of the day. You read the menu and make your choices.

But then your waiter brings your food, and you see it's just piled up on a paper plate. Your soft drink comes in a Styrofoam cup with a lid and a straw. Will you be happy to pay fine-dining prices for this meal?

You should expect a good presentation, as well as tasty food, when you go to a restaurant. A quality presentation is as much a part of your meal as the quality of the ingredients and their flavor.

Your business is no different. Bringing your A-game is about presentation. Give your customers excellence when they buy your TT&P. Give them excellence presented well. Let them see you're giving them more than they expect. Start with a quality presentation in your marketing and continue it all the way through your sales process to your follow up and asking them to be your Advocate.

What's Best for Your Customer?

Always help your customer make a decision that's a benefit to them. This means that sometimes you'll have to say, "You don't need me right now." Or you may be in a position to down-sell . . . I don't even know if that's a valid word. I think down-sell is the opposite of up-sell. Up-selling is convincing your customer to buy something better or more than they originally intended.

The most basic up-sell is when you order a burger and fries and they ask you if you want the combo meal deal. A common up-selling technique is the "extended warranty" plan. These plans are so profitable that they've expanded from appliances and electronics to things as diverse as power tools and furniture.

Down-selling is the opposite. What your customer wants isn't a good decision or it isn't in their best interests.

For example, a customer called us to refinish their cabinets. We arrived to find flimsy cabinet frames with plywood doors. We told them they should replace rather than refinish. It cost us a sale. And they were shocked.

You're frowning, I bet. You may think I've got a screw loose. Send away business? Am I crazy?

But we're not shy about up-selling either. A customer may ask for a cheaper finish that doesn't fit their high-end home. We will work to convince them of what they need: a home with unified decor.

You see, serving with excellence is a mindset. This excellence doesn't come by accident. Yes, I'm telling you to make a written plan for how to WOW your customers. But your mindset is more important than your plan. Make your customer's wants and needs more important than making a sale.

Creating your system is just a framework. Your system is there to reinforce your mindset and your core values. Your system reminds you to have your A-game on.

Your system and mindset working together will make customers love you forever.

Plan Your A-Game

Think back to times you've experienced outstanding customer service. Perhaps it was a waiter who took such good care of you. Or perhaps a store manager amazed you with a painless warranty transaction. Even small courtesies like a checkout cashier talking to you instead of mindlessly scanning your items. You remember great customer service because it's an exception. Indifference or even surly treatment is average.

It sticks in your mind when people make you feel they appreciate your business. So few businesses focus on serving their customers well that even mediocre service stands out.

You Can Be Awesome

You may not have a warm, fuzzy personality. Yes, being a "people person" is good. But some of the best customer service I ever got was from an insurance guy with a no-nonsense, get-down-to-business manner. Chitchat was not his strong suit, but he always made me feel like I was important. Whenever I called with a problem or question, he took care of it quickly. It's great when people like you. But you must deliver excellence as well.

You see, it's not about your personality. It's about your choice. Ninety-five percent of the people you meet are thinking, "I wanna talk about me!" Being self-centered comes naturally. I want the stuff I want and I want you to pay attention to me. That's the way we all are.

Set aside your own ego and your customers will love you. Pay attention to them. Listen. Hear what they say. Get over yourself and make it, "I Wanna Talk About You."

The funny thing is that if you can put aside your own need for attention and focus on them, they'll end up paying attention to you. This is how you make Advocates. Listening is more rare than rubies. Listening combined with hearing is even more rare. So if selling is serving, your serving starts by listening. Your customers will tell you what they want. If you take the time to hear, the selling is easy. And you can dazzle them too.

The Best Laid Plans

Don't throw your customer service plan in a drawer and forget about it. Set it up as a system, a Standard Operating Procedure, in your business. Practice it and follow it until it becomes a habit and your mindset. Continue the habit of serving with excellence long enough and it will become part of your personality.

One of our clients mentioned they were hesitant to hire contractors to work in their home because most are so messy. Her husband was reluctant about renovation, expecting to live for weeks with a mess. He commented that, to his surprise, the only way he knew we were even there was because of the table removed from the room and our tools put away neatly in the corner each evening. Our standard operating procedure is such a habit that I no longer think of it as exceptional. We don't make a big deal about it. We just do it. But our clients still notice.

Yes, there will be times when you won't feel like being awesome. You will run across some bozos and trolls. You'll have customers who make it next to impossible for you to serve them well. That's why I'm telling you to make yourself a system. Serve with excellence to the best of your ability. You'll have more success with some people than with others. But strive to give your A-game to everyone.

The Bad Customers

I used to see signs in stores: "We reserve the right to refuse service to anyone." Looking back now, I suspect the owners of these stores may have had racial motives. But, in some cases, they were merely saying, "If you're a jerk, I don't have to deal with you." Don't ever refuse to serve someone just because they're different — as in race or religion. But you'll find some people you can't make happy no matter what you do. Politely tell these people, "I'm sorry, but I can't help you," and walk away.

I've said it before: bad business is worse than no business. You will lose money when you have no business. Bad business will usually cost you money and suck life from your soul. Bad customers who are never happy are like leeches on your spirit. Whatever money you might make isn't worth all the crap you have to put up with.

Now I'm not saying you should grip the lever just itching to release the trap door and send your customer to Purgatory. When you make a picky customer happy, they'll be one of your best Advocates. But a customer with high expectations is a whole different animal than the one with outrageous expectations. Don't be too quick to fire a difficult customer. But, on the other hand, don't be afraid to get rid of a bad customer.

Customer Categories

Eighty percent of your customers will be impressed if you just show up and give decent service. You'll have to sort out the remaining 20%. Listen to them, and pay attention to what they tell you. You'll be able to sort them into one of three types: high-maintenance, PITA (Pain In the Ass) or Tyrants.

You can handle high-maintenance and PITA customers. Tell them what they can expect from you and then over-deliver on your promise. If your business is service-based or if you put together an estimate for your TT&P, add in a PITA charge. It's a legitimate expense to cover the hand-holding you'll have to do for these customers. Yes, you should give something extra to these people too. But there's nothing wrong with charging for the extra effort you'll put in to dazzle a picky customer.

A "Tyrant" is a customer who expects champagne quality for a beer price. These people won't be happy no matter what you give them. A Tyrant will look at the best you've got to offer and find fault with it. It's priced too high, it's not good enough, and the list goes on. Fire these customers. They are like vampires sucking away your energy and happiness.

A-Game Reputation

Finally, the important thing about showing up in the market with your A-game is that this attitude will cause you to attract a higher class of customer. Bringing your A-game will define and control the market niche you compete in. Remember our discussion about dealing with the "underbelly competition"? There's an old saying, "Don't wrestle with a pig. You'll both be covered with mud, but the pig likes mud."

You define the field of play when you bring your A-game. You're not in the mud wrestling pigs. You're not even just giving common service. You're on solid ground, serving customers who love you and rave about you to their friends.

When you give your best, you attract customers who are willing and eager to pay for the best. This is the advantage of showing up with your A-game. Working for customers who become raving fans makes being an entrepreneur fun.

Chapter 13

Growing Pains

Success will lead to a problem: you can't keep up with all the business coming in the door. You're overwhelmed. You're stressed. You're going to feel like you need to hire help.

Almost every small business owner told me this: put off hiring employees for as long as you can.

You may remember I'm encouraging you not repeat my own mistakes. My experience in hiring employees ended up a miserable failure. So what follows is my reflection on what went wrong and what I woulda-coulda-shoulda done differently.

Are You Really Ready?

Once the thought, "I should hire help" floats through your mind, slap it away like an annoying mosquito. When you can't keep it away any longer, sit down and take a good look at your business.

Ask yourself some questions: Can you train someone to do the work you do? If you're selling a service, can you find people with the level of skill you have? Can you break down what you do into pieces and create a system your employees can easily follow? If your employees need to learn skills, can you take the time away from your present business to train them?

The last question I listed is a big one. Training employees takes time. And it takes time during your productive business hours. You already have more business than you can handle. That's why you're thinking about hiring someone, right? Training an employee will slow your productivity before it increases it.

Question Mercilessly

Take a long hard look at your business. Take the list of questions above and be as brutal and honest as you can when you answer. In my case, I said yes. But I soon realized I should have looked a lot harder and deeper. I should have taken more time to consider the complexities of our business. And I should have been more pessimistic about how employees would actually fit into our business.

Our Faux Success

When faux painting was the hot decorating trend, we were swamped with work. So we hired two employees intending to create a second faux finishing team. My wife/business partner and I would each work with an employee and double the amount of work we could accomplish. This seemed like a great plan in theory. In reality, it was horrible.

Faux painting is an art. Of course when the market was hot, everyone wanted faux-finished walls. Unskilled artists flooded in to meet the demand, but they did mediocre work.

But we had honed our A-game. We served the elite, the high-end market. Our clients didn't just want paint sponged on the wall. They wanted finishes with finesse and refinement. And we had a good system in place so we could consistently deliver excellent results. Our reputation and skill level put us among the top faux finish artists in our city.

Our Faux Fiasco

We discovered "artistic vision" is neither common nor easily learned. Our two employees developed some of the technical faux painting skills, but they lacked the "eye" for the art of it.

I failed to remember that art is more than just the sum of the parts. Computer-generated music will never compare to a live performer. The notes are the same, but the art comes from the way they're put together.

Our employees learned technique, but the vision to put it together into something amazing just wasn't there. Our clients expected finesse and attention to detail. Our employees just didn't have it.

Lessons Learned

The first lesson I learned about hiring employees is this: set high standards. Don't hire employees just because you "need help." I know, you may not be hiring "artists," like I was. But your employees must buy into your business philosophy. Find that person passionate for serving people who will make your customers into raving fans.

The most successful business people hire employees more talented than themselves. So you look for passionate, talented people. Don't hire people who just want or need a job.

Write a Manual

Break down the tasks of each job. Put in as much detail as you can. List exactly what you expect and how your employees will meet those expectations. The more specific details you include, the better. Don't just hire someone and then expect him or her to learn your list of unwritten expectations. And by the way, even after you write down everything you can think of, you will still have an unwritten list of expectations.

How much do you pay?

When you bring your A-game to the marketplace, you're making a commitment to bring A-game employees along with you. This means you'll have to pay at or above the market salary for top talent. Wages for the same jobs will vary by region and the cost of living in your local marketplace.

In general, the cost of living in the US is higher on the east and west coast than in the middle of the country. Wages tend to adjust depending on the cost of living. As a general rule, the wages or salary you pay will determine how good an employee you hire. The main thing to keep in mind is to pay a wage or salary consistent with the job market in your area.

Your Overhead Goes Up

Your business budget has to change when you have employees. Your figures have to include employee salaries. You also have to cover increased overhead in the following: liability insurance, worker's comp insurance, unemployment taxes (state and federal) and your half of social security taxes as the employer.

Most business liability insurance policies are based on your payroll. The insurance company covers more risk the more employees you have, so your premiums will go up as you grow your business.

Workers comp covers your employees if they're injured on the job. Workers comp has a minimum base rate that increases the more payroll you have. Most states require you to carry worker's comp insurance when you have employees. Some states allow you to bypass worker's comp if your payroll is low enough. But you are still liable for on-the-job injuries if your employee gets hurt. Without worker's comp, you could end up paying an employee's medical bills out of your own pocket.

Unemployment and social security taxes are also based on payroll. The more money you pay out to your employees, the more taxes you'll pay. Your bookkeeping and accounting costs will go up too.

Recalculating

Plug these numbers into your business budget. Go back to your calculations for the number of hours a week and number of weeks you'll work in the field. Recalculate your rates for your TT&P. And don't forget to reduce the number of hours you're billing for your time in the field. You won't be producing or selling the same amount of your own TT&P while you're managing and training your employees.

Another Shift in Your Thinking

Expect your employees to carry their weight. The idea of hiring help is that you get more done, bring in more jobs and sell more of your TT&P. Your purpose is to bring in more money. And the only way to really grow your business is to hire people who can pull their weight. Be sure you know what you're getting into when you decide to hire employees.

Don't let my tone discourage you from taking on employees. But make sure you crunch these numbers before you do. You have to shift your thinking again when you hire employees. Entrepreneurs with employees think differently than solo entrepreneurs.

Self-employed vs. Business Owner

In the purest sense of definitions, employees make the difference between owning a business and being self-employed. You're still employed when you're self-employed. You're the entrepreneur and boss, but you still do all the work. You're not an employee in the traditional sense. You are an entrepreneur and small-business owner. But you don't get paid if you don't show up to work.

Business owners hire employees to do the work. Business owners hone and tweak their systems to run their business smoothly, even when they aren't there. They still make money, because their employees produce the TT&P.

Starting Over

The problem you have when you start your business as a solo, self-employed entrepreneur is that you go backwards for a while when you hire employees. It's like starting over in a new business.

You have to pay more in salaries and overhead. At the same time your productivity will drop because you take time away from paying jobs for training. Even when you train "on the job," you can't get as much work done. Training slows you down.

So, just like a business start up, you need cash reserves to carry you through until you're profitable again. A lot of small businesses and solo entrepreneurs languish at this roadblock for years. Some of them decide to just maintain the business they can handle rather than take the leap to the next level and hire employees.

Make a Plan

If and when you decide to make the commitment to hire employees, sit down and plan it like you planned the start of your business. Go through the same steps of analyzing your market niche, budgeting and figuring how much money you'll have to spend before your break-even point.

What I Learned from Failing

I should have planned better when I hired employees. I didn't analyze deeply enough. I didn't look at the complexities of my market or the skill level employees would need to deliver the kind of work our clients expected.

This is why I say to start with an analysis of your business. Can you hire employees with skills? There's a downside for you when you perfect your A-game: how do you find an employee as good or better than you? And, are you charging enough for your product or service to be able to pay a great employee the wages or salary he or she deserves?

In our case we decided to go back to the ranks of the self-employed. We didn't want to deal with employees any more. That decision led to the next lesson we learned: how not to fire someone.

Do It Like Trump Did

You guess it. I learned what I'm about to tell you by doing it poorly. You will need to fire an employee at some point. We should have done it sooner. We might have had success with employees if we had fired one sooner and kept looking for the talent we needed. Then again, maybe not.

When you fire someone, make it quick and direct. Be like Donald Trump in *The Aprentice*. Don't try to help your soon-to-be-former employee find a "learning experience" in this process. Let them learn their life lessons on their own.

Tell them the reasons they're not making the grade and say, "You're fired." You can use a euphemism such as "letting you go" or "no longer need your services." But make your decision and deliver it with finality and conviction. And don't second-guess yourself.

They will argue. They may be upset. But remember, you're the boss. You don't have to convince them your decision is valid. They won't see things from your point of view no matter what you say. So don't debate the reasons you give for firing them. Just give them your decision and hand them their final check. Be sure to have their final check ready so you can give it to them.

Other Alternatives

Your business isn't going to magically even out and be smooth sailing if you decide to not hire employees. You don't usually consider hiring unless your business is booming. If you're swamped, you have a good problem. But being overwhelmed all the time isn't good for your health. I prefer the stress of too much work to the worry of having too little work. But having more to do than you can get done means you've got a problem to solve. Depending on your business, you might have a couple of other options too, besides hiring employees.

Contractors

You might consider hiring contractors instead of employees. Mind you, hiring contractors won't work in every kind of business. But contractors might be a solution.

You'll have two major benefits if you hire contractors instead of employees. First, they are responsible for paying their own taxes and social security. You give contractors an IRS 1099 form at the end of the year and they deal with the government on their own.

Secondly, you don't have to keep them working when business slows down. Your obligation is only for the project or contract you made when you hired them. You don't pay unemployment taxes on their pay, and they don't get unemployment if you no longer need their service.

Now don't go getting all excited and think you can just hire people and call them contractors. Some businesses do this very thing. But you can't turn employees into contractors just by calling them by a different name. Realize that contractors are independent business people.

The IRS has rules that apply to how you hire contractors. (Are you surprised by this?) And you will have unnecessary trouble with them if you ignore their rules.

The IRS guidelines for who you call a "contractor" are in three general categories: control, money and relationship. When you hire a contractor, you have to treat them like an independent business owner because that's what they are.

You can only give them general instructions. You can't tell them how to do the job or even when to show up. And if you train them, the IRS will automatically consider them an employee. You can neither pay them benefits nor reimburse expenses. They have to have skin in the game: invest their own money and be running their own business. This includes the possibility they could lose money on a project, as well as the freedom to work for other people . . . even your competition. And you can't hire them indefinitely. They have to work on a project-by-project basis. If you're their only contract, the IRS may come knocking on your door to verify all of the above.

As you can see from these guidelines, using contractors won't work in every business. And, yes some businesses ignore these IRS guidelines. I heard of a lawn mowing service that paid their help by the hour and provided the equipment but still tried to claim their workers were contractors. Some restaurants have tried the same thing with kitchen staff and busboys.

There are always people so desperate for work they'll let employers take advantage of them. And most employees won't know the IRS rules anyway. So you might be able to get away with treating employees as contractors. But it only takes one unhappy "contractor" making the right phone call to bring the IRS to your door. This is not something you want. Remember, you want the Lord to bless and keep the Czar far away from you.

So take a good look at your business. See if it makes sense to hire independent contractors or whether you'll have to find employees. If you're like most entrepreneurs, you're probably a bit of a control freak. Giving up the ability to supervise and direct the outcome of a project may give you chills. But take a few deep breaths and calmly, honestly evaluate whether independent contractors may be the answer for growing your business . . . at least, for a while.

Raise Your Prices

The second option to consider before you hire employees is to raise your prices. Again, this option may not work for your business. It's hard to raise your rates above the market rate in your niche. Also, you may not be able to charge much of a premium. You won't sell many $20 cupcakes, no matter how good they are. But raising prices might take care of having more business than you can handle.

You'll have several benefits from raising your prices. First, it will slow your business down. I can hear you yelling at me, "What! I want more business, not less!" But remember, I'm talking about raising prices when you're at your maximum capacity — when you're running yourself ragged and have plenty of business coming in the door. You can't do more business to make more money. But if you raise your prices, your business can slow down to a manageable level. And you make more money while working less. This is a good thing.

You know about the law of supply and demand. A booming business means you're living this law. So raise your prices when your demand is high. There's a limited supply of you.

Of course, some of your customers won't pay the higher price. Don't worry. Others will pay more because they see the value you offer. Remember, you're bringing your A-game to the marketplace. When you have a premium reputation, you should charge premium prices.

Another advantage to raising your prices is you'll attract better quality customers. Remember back when I told you not to compete on price? Customers who look for value are easier to please than bargain shoppers. It seems strange, but it's true. You want customers looking for BMWs and Louis Vuitton rather than the Tata Nano, the Ford Fiesta, and Wal-mart.

Think about how luxury brands compete. They offer two things: value and exclusivity. For example, Rolex is a symbol of wealth and prestige and has been for years. This reputation comes from both the cost — they're definitely not cheap — and their reputation for being well made and stylish. They're exclusive because not everyone can afford them, and they're considered a good value because of their quality.

Luxury is Perception

When your customers perceive your value and exclusivity — you do what others can't — you can raise your prices. It is their perception that counts most. Yes, your TT&P has to be top notch. But it's your customer's belief in your value that allows you to charge more. That's why name brands sell for more than generic brands. Often, there's no practical difference in quality or performance. But customers perceive the name brand is better so they pay more.

You have a successful "name brand" when you have more business than you can handle. Raise your prices until your business is once again at a level you can manage (remember the spinning plates).

As your client base slowly shifts and you find more people willing to pay your higher prices, you'll once again find yourself overwhelmed with business. Believe me, this is a good problem to have. Do you see what you need to do? That's right. Raise your prices again.

Keep in mind, this scenario isn't going to happen overnight. But won't it be nice to be at the top of your market five years from now?

In Conclusion

Do everything you can to position your business to compete on excellent products and services. And if you do hire employees, you're going to be the one demanding excellence and performance. You need to have the mindset and attitude of excellence first. But when you hire employees, you want to be like your ideal customers -- demand quality and value. Don't go looking for cheap employees working for cheap wages. They will generally do only cheap work.

Now, you may be starting a business in which you must hire employees right away. You'll have more work and planning to do to get started. Remember that you'll have to develop yourself and your company culture . . . while at the same time getting your employees to buy into your vision for constantly improving your A-game as a company.

Chapter 14

Your Main Asset

"Anyone who stops learning is old, whether at 20 or 80. Anyone who keeps learning stays young. The greatest thing in life is to keep your mind young." - Henry Ford

You may feel overwhelmed by now. I've dumped a lot of information on you. You've done well to get this far. But you've only scratched the surface. You'll have gigabytes of information to learn, and fast, if you're thinking about making the jump from employee to entrepreneur. You're like a pioneer in a covered wagon, gazing up at the Rocky Mountains, wondering how you'll ever find your way to Oregon.

You need a pioneer spirit to make it as an entrepreneur. Don't become a settler. Don't decide the journey is too hard, and don't decide to settle for where you are. You're either growing or dying when you're an entrepreneur.

You'll be tempted to coast once your business is up and running. You lose your hunger, your pioneer spirit. Well, you can get away with coasting for a while, but know this: the only way to survive is to keep growing. Think about how a tree grows. It adds a ring each year. You want to be the same as an entrepreneur.

You're Dying if You're Not Growing

Cement this thought in your mind right now. You can't stop learning. You can't settle. Once you stop growing you're on your way to withering up and blowing away. It won't happen right away, but dying will come if you settle in and coast for long enough.

I can see you doubting me on this. Okay, let me see if I can think of an example.

Of course. Look at General Motors. I know, I know, they didn't dry up and blow away, but that's only because the US government said they were "too big to fail." Believe me, you won't have that luxury in your business.

GM had a comfortable market share in the 1960s. They had one main competitor, Ford, and a couple of lesser ones, Chrysler and American Motors. (I know you're thinking American Motors shouldn't count, but they had a tiny slice of the market back then.) All American car companies competed on luxury, horsepower and style. Twelve miles per gallon wasn't an issue when gas was cheap.

GM sneered at Toyota and the other imports when they gained a small footing in the 1970s. Even the spike in gas prices didn't change GM's attitude. They coasted along, relying on their reputation and brand recognition. They didn't really innovate. But they did try to cut their production costs, because the imports were cheaper.

What happened? GM's quality dropped and Toyota gained reputation for quality and value. So, by the turn of the century, Toyota was seen as a good value and GM was just another American car with poor gas mileage and less reliable than the imports.

So believe me. You can't settle, and you can't coast once you get your business going. You've got to keep pushing, growing and learning. The marketplace is competitive. You've got to adapt and adjust to what your customers want. Because your customers are fickle. The hot item you're selling them this year may be passé the next.

Ask Powerful Questions

So how do you keep growing? How do you keep your competitive edge as an entrepreneur? You learn how to ask powerful questions.

You see, the rules of engagement you operate and think in are set by the questions you ask. Your questions create mental boundaries you won't easily cross. Think about it this way. Present someone with two choices, A or B, and he or she will choose one of them. And most people will still choose only A or B even if both are bad.

Imagine standing at the fast food counter you're asked, "Do you want regular fries or curly fries?" You're likely to choose one of those options. They may have a salad on the menu too. But because the order taker asked you an "A or B" question, you have to concentrate to break free and say "salad."

Now you may be a health-nut and wouldn't even set foot in a hamburger joint. But you get bamboozled like this all the time. Given the choice, your brain will take the easy road every time. You accept the rules of engagement and the playing field other people lay out for you. You don't even notice. Sure, you can break this habit of "thinking along the easy road," but it takes work.

Give Me the First Right Answer

You see, your education trained you to be lazy. You are conditioned to find the first right answer. Your teachers drew the boundaries of the arena and the rules of engagement. You learned and memorized the "right answer." A few days later you had to find it again, hidden in the multiple choices of their test. Is the right answer A, B, C, or D? Once you find the right answer, you go to the next question and repeat the process. You had a time limit. So you had to find the right answers as fast as possible.

And you got a prize (a grade) based on the first right answers you found.

You learned to think inside the lines. You stopped thinking once you found the first right answer. You repeated this process, year by year, until you were fully conditioned to find the first right answer and stop there.

So now you hardly ever even consider whether the first right answer is the best answer? Perhaps there's another option that makes the first right answer irrelevant. And you never question the validity of the question. You buy into the premise and go off to find the answer.

The Rest of the Alphabet

If you had the makings of an entrepreneur, you probably looked at the answers A, B, C and D, and thought, "What about F through H?" (You skipped E because it was irrelevant.) Did you ever ask your teachers how their lessons applied to real life? Such questions brand you as a troublemaker in school. Entrepreneurs are troublemakers.

Employers don't hire such troublemakers. They want employees who give them answers to the questions they ask and stop right there. The owners and management ask the questions, and the questions define the limits of acceptable answers. They want an answer: A, B, C or D. Sometimes they want only A or B. They may tell you to "think outside the box," but they don't really mean it. You know you better toe the line, but not cross it; you better give them "safe" answers.

Don't Be Creative

Employers rarely want you to be creative. Creativity is unpredictable and messy. You better stick to proven strategies as an employee. Give the wrong answers or "creative" answers and you risk losing your job. So you learn not to ask too many questions. More specifically, you learn not to ask the wrong questions.

Just asking too many questions in general gets you labeled "not a team player."

You have to learn to play the game as an employee. Yes, your employer will ask you to "think outside the box." You know by now not to fall for it. You learn to stay in the safe boundaries of "approved out-of-the-box answers." You excel when you give acceptable answers. With practice, you learn to find the first right answers to more complex questions. Such is the path to good performance reviews and promotion in the company.

Rebel With a Cause

You've got to chuck all this out the window as an entrepreneur. You're the employer *and* the employee: the asker and the answerer. You can't be only looking for the first right answer. You've got to go looking for the most powerful question you can ask. Oh, yes. The real power is in asking questions not in finding answers.

If you ever doubt the power of questions, just consult the parent of a toddler. The simple question, "Why?" repeated by a two-year-old, can reduce the most intelligent adult to a blob of quivering Jello. At some point the parent surrenders and says the words she vowed never to say: "Because I said so!"

Powerful Questions

The power to succeed resides in the questions you ask. You see, your brain is wired to find answers. Imagine I'm sitting next to you and turn to you and ask, "Have you heard what the weather is supposed to be today?"

You may be deep in thought, but you'll stop and answer my question. Even if you're in a pissed off mood and tell me, "Buzz off," (or something worse), my question makes you stop and think about today's weather. In fact, I bet you thought about the weather just reading this paragraph.

So, as an entrepreneur, you have to learn how to ask yourself powerful questions. Because the way you ask your questions will determine the quality of the answers you get.

Remember, the person asking the question sets the boundaries and the rules of engagement. If you ask too small a question you automatically disqualify some of your best answers. You fail because you drew narrow boundaries. Your rules of engagement caged you in.

Limiting vs. Powerful Questions

In general, questions starting with "why" usually give you bad results. Just think about the "why" questions you hear: "Why did this tragedy happen? Why did that child get sick and die? Why is life so unfair? Why can't I get ahead?" And it's even worse when you ask "why" questions about yourself. Remember, your brain is wired to find answers. When you ask a "why" question about yourself, your brain is going to give you an answer.

Your answer won't be a conscious thought. Your "why" question may be a rhetorical statement rather than something you really wanted an answer to. But your brain will give you an answer. Your subconscious brain answers every question you ask.

The Elephant in the Room

Psychologists claim your subconscious mind processes terabytes of information each day. And all this data controls what you do and think. Yes, you think you're in control and being rational. But then you'll find yourself doing things you don't want. And you don't do things you really want to do.

I heard life coach Judy Rees describe the relationship of the conscious and the subconscious as an elephant trainer and an elephant. The conscious mind is the trainer. The subconscious is the elephant. If the elephant decides he doesn't want to do what the trainer asks, there's not much anyone can do to stop him.

So hold onto that metaphor and let's go back to the reason that asking why is so useless. Let's suppose you ask yourself, "Why can't I lose weight?" Your subconscious brain will answer, "Because you're a slob who eats too much and doesn't exercise."

Remember, your conscious brain doesn't really hear this answer, but you experience the emotions of defeat and humiliation as if you're subconscious brain says this out loud.

Your conscious brain says, "I should lose weight." But the elephant just ignores you. Your conscious brain loses that argument every time.

You can ask a better question: "How can I lose weight?" Your brain will give you a better answer: Put down the cupcake. Get off the couch and exercise. You don't have the same emotion of humiliation and failure with this answer. However, your subconscious still kicks in and says, "What do you mean? I love cupcakes and I don't want to exercise." Again you say, "I should lose weight." But the elephant still ignores you.

On the other hand, you can ask a powerful question: "What can I do right now to start losing weight and enjoy the process?" A question like this will set your brain — both conscious and subconscious — on a creative quest to find an answer. Asking powerful questions engages your whole brain. The elephant becomes your ally and you've got real power on your side.

When you ask a powerful question it makes your brain skip your default response and your "library of bad answers." Ask a powerful question and you get an answer that gives you a good shot at losing weight.

Your Best Asset

You might be wondering, what does this talk about your brain have to do with being self-employed? It matters a lot. Your brain is your primary asset as an entrepreneur.

At the start I talked about why you need to think differently as an entrepreneur. Your lizard brain and your employee brain are the two biggest obstacles to overcome when you start your business. But don't think for a minute you're home free. Taming your fear is only the start.

You have to keep learning if you're going to succeed as an entrepreneur. You need to keep growing. Mush forms in your brain once you settle in and slack off.

This is Your Brain on Mush

You might be able to get by with a little mush in your brain as an employee. Mush brains are lethal when you're self-employed. Believe me, your competitors lurk like wolves, waiting to snatch your customers. Your true competitors won't rest on their butts. They are out there right now, bringing their A-game. They are striving to get as much of the market share as they can.

You have no boss or a professional association pushing you to learn or take continuing education classes. You have to motivate yourself. Dig deep and push to learn how to make your A-game better.

Powerful Questions

Aren't for Wimps

I'm going on about this topic because I want you to see that powerful questions will make you grow. Don't just speed-read through this and make a mental check mark.

I'll put my hands on your shoulders and look you straight in the eye. Now that I've got your attention: *You've got to learn how to ask powerful questions. And keep learning how to ask better and better questions.*

Start with the Right Words

Remember to ask the questions who, what, when and how first. If you ever ask a "why" question, follow it up with who, what, when and how questions.

Here are some examples:

- Who do I know to give me good advice to start my business?

- What resources do I need before I start?

- When is the best time for me to start?

- How can I organize this new information to make a good decision?

- Why did that idea fail? What can I learn from the failure? How can I make a better decision next time?

I know you feel like you're standing under an information waterfall right now. Ideas are swirling and you're trying to take it all in. You're asking, "How can I remember all this stuff?"

Don't worry when you feel overwhelmed. Remember the saying, "Every journey begins with a single step." The road to being an entrepreneur may seem impossibly long right now. But as comedian Steven Wright says, "Everywhere is walking distance if you've got enough time."

And you may feel as if I'm telling you to walk all the way to Cincinnati. (If you already live there, just work with me and imagine some other destination.) No, you won't walk all the way. But you do have to take a first step. Once you get going, you'll discover resources along the way that will get you there quicker. Just take the first step and keep going.

"Try not! Do. Or do not.

There is no try." - Yoda

You're good at making lame excuses. Oh, don't get offended -- it's true. I know you make lame excuses because I make lame excuses all the time. Everyone I know makes lame excuses. "I woulda, coulda, shoulda done this or that, but . . ." It's your big BUT that keeps you stuck. If you remember the scene in Star Wars where Yoda levitates Luke's spaceship out of the muck, Luke says, "I don't believe it."

Yoda says, "That is your problem."

The way you think will determine your success or failure as an entrepreneur. The questions you ask and the mindset you develop are important because there's a good chance you're going to read this book, and probably several others, but do absolutely nothing. The reason I know this is because I've done the same thing. I've done it lots of times.

You have a dream. You want something different. You're tired of your paycheck addiction and love the idea of being an entrepreneur. And you buy books and maybe even a video course or podcasts. You're looking for the "easy button."

Hope for Sale

Advertisers know how to sell you hope. Look at the ads they use. Hope is the hook they use to sell you their stuff. You buy their product because you hope to get thin, more beautiful, get the dream boy or girl, be healthier, etc.

Hope is a powerful thing. But hope alone isn't going to get your spaceship out of the swamp. You've got to add belief and action to your hope.

Hope Without Action

I saw an endless stream of "hope buyers" when I was working my real estate investor gig. Real estate gurus told their story — rags to riches — with the promise you too could make big money if you buy their training course. I saw the same people over and over buy such "education," but they never bought any real estate. That's what hope without action looks like.

You turn hope into action by asking powerful questions. Ask powerful questions and you will get powerful answers. Now what are you going to do with those answers?

You can be like the hopeful investors, always gathering knowledge. Eventually you may be the smartest person in the room. But all the knowledge in the world won't mean jack squat if you don't take action.

"C" Students Rock

The reason so many successful entrepreneurs were poor students and dropouts is because they tend to look for knowledge they can use. Bill Gates goofed off in college. He didn't attend the classes on his schedule. He went to whatever class he felt like whether he had signed up for it or not. At the last minute, he'd cram for his tests and pass the classes on his schedule. He then dropped out of Harvard to start his little computer business.

You're it Now

I want to end with one final point: It's on you. It's the biggest shift in thinking you'll have to make as an entrepreneur. You're it. You get to choose who you will be.

The thing is, it always has been on you. Your life right now is a result of the choices you've made.

I imagine you're starting to argue with me about this. Maybe you're even a little pissed. "You don't know my life," you say.

Okay, so I don't know your life. So let me tell you how I learned this principle. My road to freedom started when I admitted that I, and I alone, am totally responsible for my life. My decisions put me right where I am.

You see, I excelled at shifting blame. I'd blame "bad luck" or circumstances beyond my control. If I couldn't shift the blame for something, I'd brush it off with, "That's just the way I am." I'd say things like, "I'm not a good planner. I'm not gifted. I'm not a type-A personality. Setting goals just isn't my thing." I was good at making lame excuses.

For years, I blamed my wife for all kinds of my problems. I would think, "If she would just . . . I could . . ."

My turning point came when someone told me the same thing I'm telling you. *You have to admit that the place you are right now is a result of all the choices you've made.*

I Am Responsible

Every decision I made had consequences. And even the "bad luck" that seemed beyond my control presented me with a choice. I chose how I responded. I chose what I thought about things that happen to me. I couldn't control my wife. But I do have a choice in how I respond to her. I always have a choice. And the choices and decisions I made along the way add up to the life I have now.

Admitting this reality made things clear. I could change my life. I just had to make different choices. I could start now and decide to become what I want to be.

I began this book by talking about your lizard brain and how fear keeps you trapped in "safe" jobs you hate. Taking responsibility for your life terrifies your lizard brain.

This lizard brain fear paralyzes you and keeps you trapped in your paycheck addiction. Fear is the reason you were arguing with me a minute ago. Your lizard brain won't admit responsibility. Responsibility feels like failure. Failure feels like danger to your lizard brain.

Step Up to the Plate

I wish I had an easy answer for you: do this one simple thing to succeed. The only way to learn this principle is to do it. You step up and take responsibility for your life, past, present and future. It's up to you.

You wake up every morning and step into the batter's box, the score tied in the ninth and two outs. And the crowd is watching. You make decisions to swing or not. You may strike out. You may hit a home run. But you're the one at bat. There's no one else to blame if you fail.

You get over your fear by seizing the bat and walking up to the plate. You can read and study and prepare until the day you die. But if you never put what you learn into action, none of that's going to do you any good.

You will never feel like you know enough. Don't wait until you're totally prepared. You won't ever start. In some ways, ignorance is bliss (for a while). In my case, I didn't know enough to be afraid. So I may risk killing your entrepreneur dreams with my stories of what I had to learn the hard way.

You may see me as unique, ignorant of danger and unafraid of risks. You think it's easy for me to now say, "Face your fear," and "Just do it." No. I've had some experience in overcoming fear. I know it's not easy.

Facing My Biggest Fear

High places used to terrify me. Balconies, glass elevators, ladders and rooftops . . . I've had embarrassing encounters with all of these because of my fear.

One day an acquaintance learned of my acrophobia and said, "I'll cure you." I was motivated. It's hard to be successful at do-it-yourself home improvements when you can't get halfway up a ladder.

My new friend took me to the top of a cliff, tied a couple of ropes around a tree, fitted us both with harnesses and after a few minutes of instruction said, "Follow me," and backed over the edge.

My death-grip on the rope didn't comfort me as I stood with 50 feet of air under my heels and my toes trying to root themselves to the rock ledge in front of me. I forced myself to lean back. My heart hammered as I tipped past the point of no return.

The stretch of the rope felt like a rubber band as the slack went out. I inched backwards down the face of that cliff, my mind racing to remember how to control my descent.

Since I'm sitting here telling you about all this, I suppose it's no surprise that I made it alive and whole to the bottom.

But I knew one and done wasn't going to cut it if I really wanted to get over my fear. So I climbed the trail to the top and did it again. Then I did it again. And again. And again.

By the time we left, I was descending the 50 feet in under two seconds, a near free-fall. My new friend was right. I was cured. I still get tense when I'm up high. But I'm no longer paralyzed by that fear.

Yes, Just Do It

My intent is for you to consider this book as your rope and harness. You can be free from your paycheck addiction. You can strap in and follow me over the edge. You can face your fear and learn to be an entrepreneur.

Of course you'll be terrified. But I can tell you it's better to know the risks and be terrified than to just blindly step off into entrepreneurship like I did.

Remember, I haven't told you everything you need to know. You never stop learning. You'll have to keep learning and growing for the rest of your life if you're going to be truly successful.

Learn to quiet your lizard brain. Learn to think like an entrepreneur and take that first step on your journey to freedom.

You have to make the decision. You don't have any guarantees. But when you take that step, you may find it's not as scary as you imagined. Believe me, once you break your paycheck addiction, you won't want to go back to being an employee.

About the Author

Eric Deeter has a home-based cabinet refinishing business in partnership with his wife, Brenda. When they aren't working in their business they're working on their "project house," the third one they've lived in during an extensive rehab. Brenda says their next rehab house will be finished before they move in.

The thirst to grow and improve pushes Eric into new projects and adventures. In his free time he's often trail running and mountain biking or on the hunt for tasty food with Brenda.

Eric also writes a blog. He writes on topics relevant to entrepreneurs running small businesses. His focus is toward the challenges faced by entrepreneurs in home-based businesses.

You can find his blog at http://ericdeeter.com.

www.ingramcontent.com/pod-product-compliance
Lightning Source LLC
Chambersburg PA
CBHW052145220526
45471CB00004B/1527